THE SIGNERS

of

THE CONSTITUTION

of

THE UNITED STATES

THE SIGNERS

of

THE CONSTITUTION

of

THE UNITED STATES

Brother C. Edward Quinn FSC

◆

With Illustrations by Reverend Thomas Ruhf CP

106 882

THE BRONX COUNTY HISTORICAL SOCIETY
THE BRONX, NEW YORK

ISBN 0-941980-18-9

THE BRONX COUNTY HISTORICAL SOCIETY
3309 Bainbridge Avenue, The Bronx, New York 10467

Editors

Gary D. Hermalyn
Lloyd Ultan

Cover and Book Design by
Henry C. Meyer, Jr.

TABLE OF CONTENTS

Brother C. Edward Quinn FSC, a member of the Brothers of the Christian Schools, is Professor of Biology at Manhattan College. He is a trustee of The Bronx County Historical Society and editor of *The Bronx County Historical Society Journal.*

◆

Thomas Ruhf is a graduate of Assumption College, Worcester, Massachussetts. He did graduate work at St. John's University in New York, and has had several exhibitions of his photographs and drawings.

INTRODUCTION

The Bicentennial of the Constitutional Convention of 1787 calls for special attention. It is more than a decade since 1976, the Bicentennial of Independence, and a year since the celebration of the hundredth birthday of the Statue of Liberty. I submit our Federal Constitution is a greater achievement than either national independence or the great lady of the harbor.

Undoubtedly a case can be made for 1987, rather than 1976, as the national bicentennial year. Between 1777 and 1789, the country was governed under the ineffective Articles of Confederation. Too attentive to the jealously independent states and too heedless of the need for national cohesion, the Articles failed to bind the country into a unified nation. United only in name after successfully winning independence, the United States floundered under the Articles, unable to conduct an effective foreign policy, establish a stable currency, or maintain national credit. Farsighted leaders, indeed everyone of sense, saw disaster ahead if the national government were not strengthened and given effectual powers.

Two events in 1786 helped emphasize the need for remedial action. One was the Annapolis Convention, called originally to resolve navigational disputes between Maryland and Virginia. Five states gathered at that meeting, and the opportunity to achieve broader gains struck several of the delegates, especially James Madison and Alexander Hamilton. The Annapolis petition to Congress led to calling a Federal Convention for Philadelphia in May of the following year. At first, the goal of the gathering was merely to revise the Articles of Confederation, but the Convention took on a life of its own, and the Federal Constitution resulted.

The second event of 1786 that impelled observant leaders to seek a stronger national government was Shays's Rebellion in Massachusetts. This nondescript but frightening tax revolt, although finally repressed with vigor by Governor James Bowdoin, showed the urgent need for reliable money and consistent laws, both dependent on a strong national government.

The delegates to Philadelphia came and went between mid-May and mid-September 1787. Some came early and enthusiastically, with carefully laid plans; others came reluctantly, wondering why they were there at all. Some stayed throughout the entire Convention; others came late, left early, or drifted in and out. Some renowned leaders refused to go at all, echoing Patrick Henry's inelegant statement that he smelled a rat. But some great men did go to Philadelphia, as did some minor talents also. Few were as determined to set up an effective national government as were Alexander Hamilton, James Madison, and James Wilson; even fewer had any plan for the shape the new government would take.

It is perhaps somewhat arbitrary to concentrate on the signers of the Constitution rather than all the delgates present at Philadelphia. It is true that some signers played minor roles at the Convention and afterwards. It is also true that several nonsigners were prominent at the convention and, subsequently, in the new nation. But the signers form a self-designated group. Even though their levels of enthusiasm for the Constitution varied, all the signers, and only the signers, formally acknowledged that the Constitution was approved by all the assembled state delegations. At the time of the signing, no state represented at Philadelphia opposed the new document, though only eleven of the thirteen were officially represented then.

It is not our intention to describe the Convention and its debates. A bibliography is provided for those who wish to pursue further study of the incredible achievement of 1787. There are also several appendices relating to the Convention and to the nonsigners that may be helpful. Our pupose is to introduce briefly each of the thirty-nine men who signed the final document, a diverse group of the brilliant and the mediocre who somehow managed to forge our national charter during that hot Philadelphia summer.

When Catherine Drinker Bowen entitled her account of the Convention *Miracle at Philadelphia*, she had it exactly right. Very few wholes have ever been so much greater than the apparent sum of their individual parts.

Brother C. Edward FSC

ACKNOWLEDGMENTS

I am grateful to all at The Bronx County Historical Society for their encouragement and assistance in preparing this little work. Special thanks, however, must go to Professor Lloyd Ultan, whose astounding knowledge of things historical is equalled only by his graciousness and good cheer, and to Dr. Gary Hermalyn, Executive Director of The Bronx County Historical Society, whose levels of creativity and enthusiasm make many good things happen. Others who provided indispensable assistance are Brother Leo Chorman FSC, Myrna Sloam D'Alessandri, Kathleen Pacher, Robert Hall, and Jeremy Geller.

THIS BOOK *follows the traditional practice of listing the signers of the Constitution in their own order of signing. The order of the biographies starts with George Washington, President of the Convention, and then continues with the other signers, geographically state by state, from north to south, with the signers of New Hampshire first and those of Georgia last.*

PRESIDENT OF
THE CONVENTION

GEORGE WASHINGTON
Virginia

February 22, 1732   *December 14, 1799*

President of the Convention

George Washington's service in winning the American Revolution, and in launching the country into the stream of nations, is well known to all. He was neither a great military strategist nor an especially creative executive. It was not Washington's ideas that made him indispensable to his country; it was his indomitability. He simply would not give up. The thought, for example, that America might actually lose the Revolution probably never entered his head.

It was precisely this determination and persistence that made Washington an effective leader. His troops knew he would never fail them, even if others did. He might not be able to do everything he wanted, but he always did all he could. By 1787, the year of the Constitutional Convention in Philadelphia, Washington was not only the greatest American leader, he symbolized a nation's confidence in itself and its hope for the future.

Reluctant as he was to leave Mount Vernon and return to public life, this great Virginian recognized perfectly well that without him the Convention had little chance for success. Despite the need to strengthen the national government, made more obvious every day by events like Shays's Rebellion in Massachusetts, the thirteen states were anything but united. None of them had any tradition of centralized national government, and many, especially in the South, regarded local affairs as vastly more important than any national union. The issue of slavery, the small states' dread of being engulfed by the large ones, the tenacious clutching of tax revenues by individual states, the squabbling over land claims in the western territories made the United States a torn cloth, more in need of reweaving than patching. Washington knew his participation in, and presiding over, the Constitutional Convention presented America with a real hope for constructing an authentic nation.

It was also necessary that Washington be the first President under the new government. His prestige was at its zenith by 1789. There were other great American leaders then, to be sure, some of them with more profound intellects than his, but the others were thought of in terms of New England, the South, or some other local region. Washington was America. He was the firm nucleus around which a nation could coalesce.

After two terms as President, George Washington died in late 1799 from the medically aggressive treatment used to cure his strep throat. He had no children of his own, though he was much devoted to the two offspring of his wife Martha by a previous marriage. George Washington was, without doubt, the one indispensable man to the American Revolution and the one indispensable man at the Constitutional Convention.

NEW HAMPSHIRE

John Langdon
Nicholas Gilman

JOHN LANGDON
New Hampshire

June 26, 1741   *September 18, 1819*

John Langdon was a wealthy merchant of Portsmouth, New Hampshire, who had been to sea as a young man, and had early taken his place among the leading Portsmouth citizens opposed to British rule. For example, he had organized and financed General John Stark's expedition against Burgoyne that ended with the victory at Bennington. Langdon himself also led militia troops from New Hampshire, and was present when Burgoyne surrendered at Saratoga.

Langdon, along with his fellow delegate Nicholas Gilman, arrived at the Constitutional Convention on July 21, when it was at the point of deciding the method of ratification. Amazingly, Langdon had been forced to provide the funds needed for himself and his other New Hampshire colleague, since the impoverished state treasury had been either unable or unwilling to advance the needed money.

Langdon supported the Constitution before the New Hampshire ratifying convention in June 1788. That convention made New Hampshire the ninth state to accept the new Federal charter, assuring that the Constitution would, in fact, go into effect.

Despite being a wealthy man with strong commercial interests, John Langdon gradually shifted his politics from Federalist to Jeffersonian, probably because of his opposition to the Alien and Sedition Laws of 1798. This transformation occurred during Langdon's two full terms in the United States Senate. When he retired in 1801, he declined President Jefferson's offer of the post of Secretary of the Navy.

After leaving the national scene, Langdon continued to be politically active at the state level. He served as Governor from 1805 to 1811, except for one year (1809), when his support for Jefferson's Embargo Act, unpopular with New England merchants and shipowners, cost him his state's chief office.

In 1812 Langdon retired completely from active public life, declining even to run for Vice-President on the ticket with James Madison.

All during his public life, and even after it, Langdon was renowned for his hospitality and entertainments. His fine old home still stands in Portsmouth, a significant component of the historic area of that town. The Langdon house effectively conveys the atmosphere of maritime New Hampshire in the era when Portsmouth was a major New England port. To see this grand old home today, with its characteristic widow's walk on the roof, is to sense once again the salt air, the seafaring men, and the anxious, waiting women that were so large a part of the New Hampshire John Langdon represented at the Constitutional Convention of 1787.

NICHOLAS GILMAN
New Hampshire

August 3, 1755   *May 2, 1814*

Nicholas Gilman was a relatively obscure member of a prominent New Hampshire family. He had served honorably during
the Revolution, but without achieving any great fame. He is,
perhaps, rather typical of New Hampshire's attitude toward the
Constitutional Convention. For one thing, New Hampshire provided no funds to cover the expenses of her delegates to Philadelphia. Consequently, even though Gilman had been named, he
did not reach Philadelphia until July 21, after most of the crucial
work had already been done. And neither Gilman nor his fellow
delegate, John Langdon, would have got there at all, had not
Langdon, a prosperous Portsmouth merchant, covered the expenses of both men. When Gilman and Langdon arrived, however,
they went right to work, and New Hampshire's vote is recorded

in James Madison's diary for July 23 as *no* on submitting the Constitution to the state legislatures for ratification and *aye* on submitting the Constitution to assemblies chosen in the states by the people.

There is an irony involved in the New Hampshire delegation's arriving just barely in time to vote on the mode of ratification. The Convention later decided that the new Constitution would become operative once it had been ratified by nine states. As fate would have it, New Hampshire was the ninth state to ratify. While all eyes were on New York and Virginia, New Hampshire ratified on June 21, 1788, after an earlier state convention, composed of uninformed delegates, unsure of what they were expected to do, had adjourned without even voting.

Gilman served in Congress from 1789 to 1797 as a Federalist. By 1802, however, he had become a Jeffersonian Democrat, probably in reaction to a falling out with his brother, John Taylor Gilman, who had been elected Federalist Governor of New Hampshire in 1794. As a Democrat, Gilman was elected to the Senate in 1804. He served there until his death, on the way home to Exeter after a session of Congress.

Nicholas Gilman exemplifies a phenomenon often noted in the pre-Constitution Congress, as well as in the selection of delegates to the Convention itself. In several states, the political emphasis was on the local scene. The primary focus of New Hampshire's governmental concern was the state itself. Lesser men went to Congress or to the Constitutional Convention. It does no injustice to Gilman to point out that there were more prominent New Hampshire leaders than he, but they were not then especially interested in a national government. Such an interest developed later. Yet Gilman served capably; certainly his eight years in the House of Representatives and ten in the Senate were major contributions from a willing man at a formative period when his country needed all the generous support it could muster.

MASSACHUSETTS

Nathaniel Gorham
Rufus King

NATHANIEL GORHAM
Massachusetts

May 1738   *June 11, 1796*

Although Nathaniel Gorham is not now well known to Americans, this Charlestown, Massachusetts, merchant played a major role at the Constitutional Convention. In order to conduct its business informally, and to take nonbinding votes, the Convention often resolved itself into a Committee of the Whole. By this parliamentary device, the presiding officer of the assembly yielded his chair to an elected chairman, who then presided over the body's discussions unregulated by the usual parliamentary rules. In the Committee of the Whole, the Convention's members felt free to change sides until their views were clarified and their positions fairly well decided. The Committee of the Whole could recommend actions, but could make no decision binding on the assembly. It was a useful device for facilitating preliminary discussion of the issues that the Convention faced.

On May 30, just a few days after the Convention had begun, Nathaniel Gorham was elected chairman of the Committee of the Whole, presiding as long as the informal rules were in effect. It is probable that Gorham, a Massachusetts delegate, received this post as a courtesy to New England, which had supported the Virginian, George Washington, for the presidency of the Convention.

After the Philadelphia sessions had ended, Gorham led a moderately distinguished public career. He supported the new Constitution at the Massachusetts ratifying convention, which approved the national compact on February 5, 1788, the sixth state to do so. At this ratifying convention, Gorham joined several other noted Massachusetts patriots, most significantly John Hancock and Samuel Adams, in gaining a narrow victory for ratification by a vote of 187 to 168. Most of Gorham's public service after 1787, however, was at the state level. For example, he was a member of the State Council, a sort of state senate, from 1788 to 1789.

Unhappily, like many others, especially James Wilson and Robert Morris among the delegates to the Constitutional Convention, Nathaniel Gorham had invested heavily in land, hoping to

resell at a large profit. In 1788 he and a partner bought 6,000,000 acres of land in Genesee County, New York. Later in the same year, Gorham and his partner purchased 2,600,000 more acres. They were ultimately unable to keep up their payments, and had to surrender their claims, losing both the land and the money already invested.

Financial failure dogged the last years of Gorham's life. He died of a stroke in 1796, less than a decade after his distinguished service at Philadelphia.

RUFUS KING
Massachusetts
March 24, 1755   *April 29, 1827*

Rufus King, one of Massachusetts' most distinguished lawyers and political leaders, came to the Convention with impressive credentials. He had served in the Continental Congress in 1784-1786, making a name for himself in 1785 by introducing the prohibition of slavery into the Northwest Ordinance, which finally passed in 1787. Curiously enough, however, by the time King came to Philadelphia as a Massachusetts delegate, he had already moved to New York in order to better the opportunities for his law career.

Relatively few delegates to the Constitutional Convention underwent any major change in their fundamental view of what the Convention should do; King was one who did. When he arrived in Philadelphia, he favored merely revising the Articles of Confederation. The debates soon persuaded him of the need to discard the old Articles entirely, and to replace them with a strong central government.

Rufus King must have been an impressive figure at the Convention. Delegate William Pierce of Georgia, among his vignettes of his fellow delegates, described King as "high in the confidence and approbation of his Country-men." But Pierce had some reservations all the same. "His [King's] action is natural, swimming, and graceful, but there is a rudeness of manner sometimes accompanying it." Yet King comes off all right in Pierce's final assessment: "But take him *tout en semble*, he may with propriety be ranked among the Luminaries of the present Age."

Pierce had that correct. Rufus King continued his career with great distinction indeed. Under the new Federal government, King served a six-year term as a Senator from New York. In 1796, President Washington appointed him Minister to Great Britain. In 1804 he ran as the Federalist candidate for Vice President under General Charles Cotesworth Pinckney of South Carolina. In 1816, as the Federalist presidential candidate, King lost the election to James Monroe, a protégé of Jefferson and Madison.

King publicly opposed the Missouri Compromise of 1820 because it would admit Missouri to the Union as a slave state. Instead, he advocated selling public lands in order to raise funds for emancipating the slaves and compensating their owners.

This distinguished statesman lived the last years of his life in Jamaica, Queens, and his home there still exists. Indeed, King lies buried in the nearby graveyard of Grace Episcopal Church. One of his sons, John Alsop King, served a term as Governor of New York (1857-1859).

CONNECTICUT

W.ᵐ Sam.ˡ Johnson

Roger Sherman

WILLIAM SAMUEL JOHNSON
Connecticut

October 7, 1727   *November 14, 1819*

William Samuel Johnson presents a puzzling case indeed. It is true that this Stratford, Connecticut, lawyer, later to become President of Columbia College in New York (1787-1800), was active in opposing the Stamp Act of 1765, served as Connecticut Colonial Agent in London, and supported the colonial nonimportation agreements of the 1760s against Great Britain. But it is also true that Johnson declined to serve in the First Continental Congress (1774), that he fell into disfavor with Connecticut Whigs during the Revolution for what they regarded as the tepidity of his patriotic ardor, and that he was arrested in 1779, only to be released by Governor Jonathan Trumbull upon Johnson's taking the oath of allegiance to the American cause.

Somehow, these clouds seem to have cast neither long nor very dark shadows over Johnson's career. He served in Congress from 1784 to 1787 under the Articles of Confederation, and became one of Connecticut's three delegates to the Constitutional Convention.

At Philadelphia Johnson played a major role. The Connecticut Compromise, introduced by Roger Sherman on June 11, was the key proposal that broke the logjam produced by the opposed positions of the large and the small states. The former insisted on representation in the national legislature according to population; the latter demanded equal representation for each state, regardless of population. The Great Compromise proposed equal representation in one house and proportional in the other. There were details to iron out, but the Convention was able to move ahead once again with real hopes for ultimate success.

A further significant role played at the Convention was Johnson's participation in the Committee on Style, which actually wrote the Constitution in its final form. The real penman was Gouverneur Morris, but as Chairman of the Committee, Johnson played a prominent part in approving the final draft.

Most of William Samuel Johnson's later life was devoted to the leadership of Columbia College, now Columbia University,

but he did serve two years as a Connecticut Senator under the new Constitution (1789-1791). Johnson had also been active in winning Connecticut's ratification of the Federal Constitution on January 8, 1788, making it the first New England state to accede to the Federal compact. He died in 1819, just a month and a week after his 92nd birthday. No other signer of the Constitution reached so advanced an age.

ROGER SHERMAN
Connecticut

April 30, 1721   *July 23, 1793*

It is probably unfair to Roger Sherman to describe him as a shoemaker who became a lawyer and a political leader. He really was an extremely hard worker who started life as the son of a hardscrabble Massachusetts farmer. With no formal education, he trained himself as a cobbler, a surveyor, a retail merchant, a lawyer, and the New Milford representative to the General Assembly of Connecticut. After moving to New Haven in 1761, he became treasurer of Yale (1765-1766) and a member of the Superior Court of Connecticut (1766-1789).

Delegate William Pierce of Georgia, not otherwise prominent at the Constitutional Convention, jotted down impressions of his fellow delegates, including Sherman. The Connecticut leader, one of six men to sign both the Declaration of Independence and the Federal Constitution, is described by Pierce as "awkward, unmeaning, and unaccountably strange in his manner. But in his train of thinking there is something regular, deep, and comprehensive; ...no man has a better heart or a clearer head."

On June 11, 1787, Sherman displayed his clear head by introducing the famous Connecticut Compromise into the Convention. This proposal provided for one house of Congress to be elected according to population, and the other to give equal representation to each state, regardless of size. In its original form, each state would have had only one senator. Later, of course, this number was increased to two.

Although the Connecticut Compromise was not exclusively Sherman's accomplishment, and it was at first rejected by the Convention, he did, in fact, effectively advocate its eventual adoption. It is entirely possible that this proposal was the most important one made at the Convention, for it broke up the impasse between the smaller states that wanted equal representation in the national legislature and the larger states that insisted on proportional representation. The small states, of course, feared that proportional representation would give the larger states enough legislative votes to ride roughshod over the interests of the small ones.

Sherman, not surprisingly, strongly supported the ratification of the new Constitution by Connecticut on January 8, 1788, the fifth state to do so. He subsequently served in both the House of Representatives and the Senate of the new national government. His political views were conservative and Federalist, yet there are two statements about him that are especially appealing. One statement, by Federalist Fisher Ames, noted that whenever Ames had been unable to attend discussions of a bill, he always felt safe by simply voting as Sherman did. The other tribute is from Thomas Jefferson, whom no one ever accused of being a Federalist. Jefferson once pointed to Sherman as one who "never said a foolish thing in his life."

NEW YORK

Alexander Hamilton

ALEXANDER HAMILTON
New York

January 11, 1757   *July 12, 1804*

Almost everything about Alexander Hamilton is astounding. He was born out of wedlock in Nevis, British West Indies, but he went to a select school in Elizabethtown, New Jersey, in 1772; he entered Columbia College in 1773; he was an influential political pamphleteer by 1774; and, when the Revolutionary War broke out in 1775, he was only eighteen. Such a rise could well be described as meteoric.

Hamilton was not reticent about his talents either. In 1776 he commanded an artillery battery with the rank of captain. In 1777 he became a military aide to Washington, assisting significantly in several reorganizations of the Continental Army.

Hamilton's self-confidence, his unquestionable genius, and his prominence in the Army put him in touch with almost every important American of his time. He corresponded extensively with Gouverneur Morris, Robert Morris, Robert Livingston, and innumerable others. In 1780 he married Elizabeth, daughter of General Philip Schuyler, thus placing himself in the uppermost rank of New York society. Even a subsequent falling-out with Washington (February 1781) did not seriously dim his luster.

Hamilton showed up at the Constitutional Convention with strong views about a powerful and effective government. In fact, his views were so monarchical and pro-British that he alienated most of his colleagues. He also had another problem at Philadelphia: as a member of the New York delegation, he was under instructions to participate only in revising the Articles of Confederation. The other two New York delegates, John Lansing and Robert Yates, took these instructions seriously. When the Convention moved toward writing a new Constitution, they returned home. So did Hamilton for a time, and even when he came back, sitting alone, he could hardly claim to represent New York in any official capacity. That fazed him not at all, nor did it silence him in the debates.

Hamilton's great Constitution triumph came after adjournment in Philadelphia. The anti-Constitution forces at the New York ratifying convention in Poughkeepsie, under the leadership of the seldom heard Governor George Clinton and the seldom

silent Melancton Smith, held a preponderance of the votes when the sessions began. In what must surely be one of the greatest feats of vote swaying in American history, Hamilton and his allies swung the New York ratifying convention from an estimated 2 to 1 opposition to a narrow 30 to 27 victory for the new Federal Constitution. No small part of this victory can be attributed to Hamilton's brilliant contributions to *The Federalist,* a forceful pamphlet co-authored by Madison and John Jay, which cogently set forth the philosophy, mechanisms, and prospects of the national government.

Hamilton, as first Secretary of the Treasury, brought his centralist views into the new government, setting a precedent, along with Washington himself, for strong national leadership.

Hamilton's genius never slackened until snuffed out in a duel with Aaron Burr on July 11, 1804. So gigantic was Hamilton's role in the founding of the nation that his equally gifted archrival Thomas Jefferson called him "a host unto himself." You did not need many other enemies if Hamilton was against you; you needed few other allies if he was on your side.

NEW JERSEY

Wil Livingston
David A Brearley.
Wm Paterson.
Jona: Dayton

WILLIAM LIVINGSTON
New Jersey

November 1723   *July 25, 1790*

William Livingston was one of the oldest delegates to the Constitutional Convention. Only Franklin and Roger Sherman were older, and Maryland's Daniel of St. Thomas Jenifer was the same age. Since Livingston belonged to the famous New York family, he possessed plenty of political clout. But before the Revolution, the Livingstons were endlessly engaged in political feuds with the Tory De Lanceys of New York City. During a period of De Lancey ascendancy, Livingston moved to Elizabethtown (now Elizabeth), New Jersey, to try his luck as a lawyer and politician in a different state.

Tall, extremely thin, and rather graceless in bearing, William Livingston had been Governor of New Jersey since 1776 when he arrived at the Convention. William Pierce described him as "confessedly a Man of first rate talents, but he appears to me rather to indulge in a sportiveness of wit, than a strength of thinking."

Governor Livingston was not, despite Pierce's view of him, a frivolous joker. In fact, he chaired a Convention committee whose role was to try to harmonize conflicting North and South views on export and import duties, and on the slave trade. Livingston reported for his committee the recommendation that slave importation not be forbidden before 1800, that their importation not be taxed at a greater rate than the average duties laid on other imports, and that any navigation act passed by Congress would require only a majority vote for passage, not a two-thirds margin. This does not sound like an especially noble bit of statesmanship, but, placed in perspective, it was one of several compromises reached at Philadelphia, the absence of which could have caused the collapse of the Convention and the loss of the chance to form a nation.

The Livingstons, especially from the standpoint of colonial New York politics, were often referred to as "Presbyterians." The De Lanceys and their allies were "Anglicans." These terms had less to do with religion than with politics. The Livingstons were

Presbyterians mainly in the sense of being opposed to the established Anglican Church. The DeLanceys were Anglicans largely because that was the side on which their political bread was buttered. Indeed, after his death in 1790, Livingston was actually interred at Trinity Episcopal Church on Wall Street. By that time, the former meanings attached to the terms Presbyterians and Anglicans no longer had any validity.

William Livingston played another role in the American Revolution that is not often remembered. When fifteen-year-old Alexander Hamilton came to America from the West Indies in 1772, he stayed with Livingston at Elizabethtown. Whether or not this environment actually made a Whig out of Hamilton, it certainly exposed him to the ideas of one of New Jersey's more active advocates of freedom.

Livingston supported the Consitution at the New Jersey ratification convention which, on December 18, 1787, unanimously voted its approval, making New Jersey the third state to ratify, and the last one to do so in 1787, the year of the Constitutional Convention itself.

DAVID BREARLEY
New Jersey

June 11, 1745   *August 16, 1790*

David Brearley was a Trenton lawyer who, in 1779, became Chief Justice of New Jersey. He had been active in the Revolution from 1776 to 1779, serving as Lieutenant Colonel in the Fourth and First New Jersey militia. Brearley was also a member of the New Jersey state constitutional convention of 1776.

Like the rest of the New Jersey delegation at the Federal Constitutional Convention in Philadelphia, Brearley was extremely wary of the power of large states like Virginia and Pennsylvania. He feared that, if given proportional representation in the new national legislature, they would utterly swamp the small state interests. Under the Articles of Confederation, each of the thirteen states had a single vote in Congress, and Brearley wanted the new Constitution to preserve that arrangement.

An interesting facet of the Constitutional Convention is the number of now relatively unknown men among its delegates. Surely it is not unfair to consider David Brearley one of these. He was well known in New Jersey in 1787, yet who would remember him today if he had not put his signature to the Constitution? However, even if he stood in the shadow of giants, Brearley was much in evidence during the Philadelphia sessions. His attendance was regular and he participated in the debates. His most notable intervention came on June 9, when in supporting William Paterson's New Jersey Plan on the floor, Brearley proposed that "a map of the United States be spread out, and that all the existing boundaries be erased, and that a new partition of the whole be made into 13 equal parts." The Convention was not ready for that, of course, and a better way out of the big state-small state problem was presented two days later when Roger Sherman offered the Connecticut Compromise.

David Brearley's life was tragically short, for he survived the Constitutional Convention by only three years, dying in 1790 at the age of 45. But he had one more major public service left before his early death. He presided over the New Jersey ratifying convention which assented to the Federal Constitution on December 18, 1787.

WILLIAM PATERSON
New Jersey
December 24, 1745   *September 9, 1806*

William Paterson, born in County Antrim, Ireland, was brought to America as an infant in 1747. He was educated through the M.A. degree at the College of New Jersey (now Princeton), and studied law under Declaration of Independence signer Richard Stockton.

In 1775 Paterson was elected a deputy to the New Jersey Provincial Congress, and in 1776 he was named to the state constitutional convention. In that same year he became Attorney-General of New Jersey.

William Paterson was one of the major figures at the Constitutional Convention at Philadelphia. It was not so much what he did, for his plan never carried, but he launched a well planned assault on behalf of the small states against proportional representation as the basis for seating delegates to the new national legislature, not yet called Congress. Paterson wanted each state, regardless of population, to possess just one vote.

Up until Paterson's intervention, the Convention had been deliberating on the Virginia Plan as reported by the Committee of the Whole on June 13. Paterson moved the New Jersey Plan on June 15, differing fundamentally from the Virginia Plan in calling for equal state representation and in retaining far more of the loose central government of the old Articles of Confederation. Both the Virginia Plan and the Connecticut Compromise had been debated before Paterson's new plan went to the floor. The Compromise had been set aside at first, but its return was really necessitated by this head-on collision that threatened the collapse of the whole Convention.

Despite the trouble it caused at the time, Paterson's motion undoubtedly worked for the long-term good. Without it, a problem that was solved in Philadelphia might have festered unresolved for years, even if some national form of government had been accepted.

Paterson, for whom, of course, Paterson, New Jersey, is named, supported the Constitution in its final form before the New Jersey ratifying convention. He served as a Senator from his state

for one year, resigning to accept the governorship of New Jersey upon the death of William Livingston in 1790.

In 1793 Paterson was named to the United States Supreme Court by President Washington. While on the bench, he presided over the trials of several leaders of the Whiskey Rebellion of 1794, and of Congressman Matthew Lyon under the Sedition Act of 1798.

Ill health induced this signer to travel to Ballston Springs, New York, in 1806. His journey produced no cure, however, and he died in Albany at the home of his daughter, Cornelia, wife of Stephen van Rensselaer.

JONATHAN DAYTON
New Jersey
October 10, 1760   *October 9, 1824*

If the name seems familiar, you are probably thinking of Dayton, Ohio. And this city is indeed named for Jonathan Dayton, youngest signer of the Constitution, who did not reach his 27th birthday until nearly a month after the Convention had adjourned. Young Dayton had served in the Revolution from 1776 until its end, holding the rank of Captain at Yorktown. Despite this service, he reached the Convention in 1787 through a sort of back door: his far better known father, Elias, had been appointed, but the elder man declined in favor of his son.

Jonathan proved an obdurate supporter of the small states' position on representation in the national government. In fact, he would have no part in any compromise on the matter. Pierce describes him as possessing "an impetuosity in his temper that is injurious to him"; but there was also "an honest rectitude about him that makes him a valuable Member of Society...." Pierce adds the fact that he and Dayton had served together as aides to General John Sullivan in the 1779 expedition against the Iroquois.

Dayton did well under the new Constitution, despite his earlier opposition. He was a member of the Second, Third, and Fourth Congresses, and Speaker of the House in the Fifth. He served in the Senate from 1799 to 1805, and supported President Jefferson's Louisiana Purchase of 1803. In the impeachment trial of Supreme Court Justice Samuel Chase of Maryland, a signer of the Declaration of Independence, Senator Dayton voted *not guilty* on all eight counts.

It is unfortunate to have to add here that Jonathan Dayton, who seemed to have served his country so well and in such distinguished offices, fell victim to the lure of western land speculation. He appears to have been involved with Aaron Burr's dubious, if ill-defined, dealings with Spain and France. Just what Burr was trying to achieve is not clear even now, though he seemed willing to strike a deal with the European powers in exchange for personal territorial and political gains. Dayton did not follow Burr very far in these quasi-treasonous dealings, but

far enough to be indicted for high treason in 1807. The charges were later dismissed, but the cloud over Dayton never entirely dissipated. He died in 1824, and his death has been attributed to exhaustion following his great exertions in honoring Lafayette when the Marquis returned to the United States in that year. It is sad indeed to look at Dayton's life and see so bright a star dimmed and tarnished in its final years.

PENNSYLVANIA

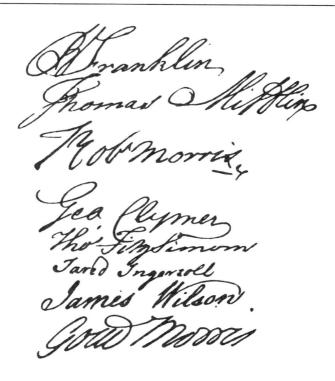

BENJAMIN FRANKLIN
Pennsylvania

January 17, 1706   *April 17, 1790*

Shrewd, experienced, ingratiating Ben Franklin dispensed kind words, trenchant witticisms, and practical wisdom to the delegates at the Constitutional Convention. His age and physical debilities kept Franklin largely silent during the actual sessions, and when he did wish to speak, James Wilson often read his interventions. But Franklin never stopped talking at home, in his garden, at his tea table, at the chessboard, or over a glass of wine. Being the oldest man at the Convention had its advantage: people listened to him.

Franklin believed that his ideas could get lost in the clamor of debate, but would slowly sink in if injected through amiable conversation. And what were his ideas? Well, they were a little more democratic, or liberal as we would probably say today, than what the Constitution eventually embodied. Franklin would have preferred a single legislative house based on proportional representation, along with a weak executive. But even this stance proved useful. Franklin acquiesced to the document the Convention ultimately produced, duly noting that, although the Constitution seemed imperfect to him, it might indeed prove excellent when tested by time. Furthermore, he believed it unlikely that any better document could be produced in the America of that day. When Franklin, whose views were well known, made statements like that, others found themselves willing to relinquish their own objections as well.

Franklin's support of the Constitution significantly enhanced its chances for ratification. A world authority on electricity, an experienced and skillful diplomat, and a lionized social luminary, Franklin was a magnet that drew other minds to his. There was no American who approached him as a statesman. From the Albany Plan of Union in 1754, through the great years of service as American Minister to France, Franklin was always in full view on the national and international stage. In London he had represented such diverse colonies as Massachusetts, Pennsylvania, and Georgia. He had taught himself to read French, Italian, Spanish, and Latin; he had learned to speak French with a carefully cultivated American homespun flavor. He was known to all the world, and admired by nearly everyone.

But fame and wealth had not always been Franklin's lot. Born in poverty, and a runaway at sixteen, Franklin was an ingenious promoter and organizer who had struggled to the top of Philadelphia's élite before he tackled the larger world. Even in his years of greatest acclaim, Franklin was dogged by misfortune. An especially poignant episode was the estrangement from his son William; once the closest of companions, the two Franklins divided over loyalties during the Revolution. William was the last royal governor of New Jersey, a post he had gained with considerable paternal assistance, and he paid for it. Without protest from his father, who considered him a traitor, Governor Franklin went to prison and to exile. To the author of *Poor Richard's Almanac*, blood was thicker than water only if the blood was loyal and true.

Franklin's long life, which touched so many people in so many lands, ended in Philadelphia on April 17, 1790. No American of his time was more highly revered. His prestige and tact had done much to win acceptance of the Constitution by a divided nation still groping to find its way along uncharted paths.

THOMAS MIFFLIN
Pennsylvania

January 10, 1744   *January 20, 1800*

Thomas Mifflin may be the most perplexing of the delegates to the Constitutional Convention. He was born in Philadelphia into the family of a prosperous merchant. He attended the College of Philadelphia, traveled in Europe, and entered business with his brother. The young man was active in politics also, and attended the First Continental Congress in 1774.

All this is more unusual than it might seem, for Mifflin, who was from a Quaker family, was a Whig who favored war with England. This unacceptable attitude led to his expulsion from the Society of Friends in 1775.

During the Revolution, Mifflin's record is even more puzzling. He served as an aide-de-camp to General Washington, and later as Quartermaster-General of the Continental Army. Yet he was involved in the Conway Cabal of 1777-1778, a movement to oust Washington as Commander-in-Chief, and to replace him with General Horatio Gates. Furthermore, Mifflin's management of the quartermaster service was so bad that he had to resign his position in 1778.

Happily for him, Mifflin was a "survivor." Neither his failures in responsible positions nor his hot and cold support of Washington seems to have seriously disabled him politically. In 1778-1779 he served in the Pennsylvania Assembly, and in 1782-1784 he sat in Congress. In fact, in 1783-1784, he was President of Congress, and accepted Washington's resignation as Commander-in-Chief of the Continental Army.

At the Convention of 1787, Mifflin sided with the large states' men, and supported the new Constitution. He chaired the Pennsylvania state constitutional convention in 1789-1790, and from 1790 to 1799, he held the office of governor of his state.

But the last years of Governor Mifflin's life were spotty. For example, in 1794, he at first sympathized with the rebellious farmers of the Whiskey Rebellion, and later came to support their suppression only with great reluctance. This was a curious position for one who had helped formulate the very Constitution to

which the Whiskey Rebellion was so fundamental a challenge.

Thomas Mifflin presents us with the perplexing, almost contradictory picture of a Quaker who was a soldier, a friend of Washington who conspired against him, and a proponent of the Constitution who only reluctantly brought himself to support it in a time of need.

Ultimately, Thomas Mifflin's inconsistencies merged into personal disaster. While still governor, he began a precipitous moral and physical decline that resulted largely from excessive drinking. He died penniless in Lancaster in 1800, still relatively young, but a pathetic case of inconsistent performance and unfulfilled possibilities.

ROBERT MORRIS
Pennsylvania

January 31, 1734   *May 8, 1806*

Robert Morris was a man of finances. His genius at making a penniless Congress look as though it really could pay its bills had served America well during the Revolution. While money would indeed be important to the United States under the Federal Constitution, at the Convention of 1787 it was really not a major item. Furthermore, Morris had been displaced by a rising star in the financial firmament, Alexander Hamilton.

Therefore, Morris, though a well known patriot, did not play a major role in the Convention itself. He did serve as host to George Washington, however, and this gave him access to the General's ear. It also placed Morris in constant touch with other delegates who paid informal visits to Washington after business hours. Morris later supported ratification not only in Pennsylvania, but also in Virginia, when he found himself in Richmond on a business trip while the Old Dominion state was debating whether to accept the new Constitution.

Morris, who was born in England, had come slowly to the idea of American Independence. This may have been because his business relied heavily on trade with England. In any case, Morris was so uncertain of the wisdom of separation that when independence came to a vote on July 2, 1776, he absented himself from the session. But once Morris had decided, his commitment was substantial and unswerving. On numerous occasions he raised money for Congress on his personal credit alone. And more than once he had to make good the debt out of his own pocket.

Maybe it is unavoidable that a public servant perceived as wealthy will arouse suspicion among his rivals. Morris experienced this distrust. In 1779 he was accused of wartime profiteering. In a development strikingly suggestive of contemporary goings on, a Congressional investigation was held at Morris's insistence, and he was exonerated.

There is an even more unhappy note to the career of this corpulent, naturally jovial man. His financial genius abandoned

him and a reckless opportunism seized him when he thought of the lands of the Northwest Territory. Morris foresaw, accurately enough, that one day those lands would be invaluable. When they did not appreciate in value quickly enough, however, Morris found himself saddled with debts he could not pay. He consequently spent three years in debtors' prison (1798-1801). Though not all his friends abandoned him, and even Washington visited him, Robert Morris's spirit was broken. When he died in 1806, he closed his life under a shadow. If not totally disgraced, for nobody ever charged him with having stolen the money he could not repay, Morris was at least discredited. It seems a sad end for one of only six men to sign both the Declaration of Independence and the Federal Constitution.

GEORGE CLYMER

Pennsylvania

March 16, 1739   *January 24, 1813*

George Clymer, one of six who signed both the Declaration of Independence and the Federal Constitution, was orphaned before his first birthday. Raised by an uncle, Clymer began his business career as a clerk, and ultimately rose to partnership in one of Philadelphia's largest merchant houses.

George Clymer was a captain of volunteers during the Revolution, a member of the Pennsylvania Council of Safety, and one of the first Continental Treasurers. In 1776 he was elected to the Continental Congress, arriving in time to sign the Declaration of Independence, but not soon enough to vote on independence itself. In fact, Clymer along with four other Pennsylvania delegates were actually sent to Congress to replace those members of the Pennsylvania delegation who had opposed independence.

There must have been something tactful and discreet about George Clymer, for he seemed frequently to receive assignments requiring diplomacy and a delicate touch. For example, in 1776 he was appointed to a commission to inspect the northern Continental Army, a jealousy-ridden and intrigue-filled command if ever there was one. In the following year, he served on a committee reviewing the activity of the army commissariat, another hotbed of self-seekers with tender sensitivities. Later still, in 1777, Clymer functioned on a committee investigating the causes of disaffection, and perhaps treason, in western Pennsylvania.

Although active in public life, Clymer had no burning political ambitions of his own. He was much interested in commercial development and public philanthropy, but he held public office only reluctantly and briefly. He preferred to expend his energies on projects like reforming the penal code of Pennsylvania, directing the Philadelphia Bank, presiding over the Academy of Fine Arts, and promoting the Philadelphia Agricultural Society.

At the Federal Convention Clymer had little to say. He was not active in the floor debates, but he did serve on a select committee to work out an agreement on the regulation of foreign trade. This group dealt with a more fundamental problem than commerce, however, for part of its charge concerned the slave trade. Chairman William Livingston of this commitee reported a compromise in which the importation of slaves would not be forbidden before 1800, and the imported slaves would not be taxed at a rate higher than the average duties laid on other imports. Furthermore, any navigation act would require only a simple majority in Congress, not the two-thirds vote previously agreed to. These may seem like strange agreements now, but failure to achieve them then could have led to the collapse of the whole Convention.

George Clymer served a term in the new House of Representatives, showing generally Jeffersonian political principles, though he personally possessed great admiration for George Washington. Toward the end of his life, Clymer belonged to the Friends Meeting in Trenton, New Jersey, just across the Delaware River from his Morrisville, Pennsylvania home. This Founding Father, well known and highly respected in his own day is, unfortunately, little remembered now.

THOMAS FITZSIMONS
Pennsylvania

1741   *August 26, 1811*

Irish-born Thomas FitzSimons was one of Philadelphia's principal merchants at the time of the Federal Constitutional Convention. Interestingly, FitzSimons's partner and brother-in-law was George Meade, grandfather of the Union general of that name who achieved victory for the North at Gettysburg.

FitzSimons served in the militia, and later in Congress, during the Revolution. Near the end of the war, he and his partner contributed about $5,000 of their firm's money toward the maintenance of the Continental Army.

At the Constitutional Convention, FitzSimons was an active advocate of a strong national government, and of restricted suffrage and office-holding qualifications. After the Convention, he served three terms in the first House of Representatives. In this Congress, he supported Alexander Hamilton's plan to retire the national debt, as well as a protective tariff to encourage American manufacturing.

Like several of the Constitution signers, FitzSimons had major financial investments to protect. He saw a strong central government as the best means for safeguarding property and securities. Also, like other Constitution signers, FitzSimons was much involved in the life of his community. In addition to being a founder of the Bank of North America, he was founder and director of the Insurance Company of North America, and President of the Philadelphia Chamber of Commerce. Furthermore, he served many years as trustee of the University of Pennsylvania, belonged to the Hibernian Society in Philadelphia, and helped build St. Augustine's Church in that city. Thomas FitzSimons was well known both as a philanthropist and as a business leader.

After the ratification of the Constitution, Philadelphia held a grand Fourth of July celebration that included a Federalist procession. Among the features of the procession was Thomas FitzSimons, representing the French Alliance, mounted on a horse that had once belonged to the Comte de Rochambeau. FitzSimons carried a white silk flag bearing three *fleurs de lys* and thirteen

stars. Other Pennsylvania signers in the same procession, even if not so ornately accoutred, included Thomas Mifflin and George Clymer.

It is true that Thomas FitzSimons was a minor character in the Constitutional panorama. At no time was he a leader in either the Convention debates or the document's formulation. But he supported it, promoted it among the merchant class, and played his small part loyally and effectively. He died in 1811, approximately 70 years of age.

JARED INGERSOLL
Pennsylvania

October 27, 1749   *October 31, 1822*

Jared Ingersoll was a Connecticut native who had moved to Philadelphia in 1778, after two years' living in Europe. As befitted a New Haven man, Ingersoll had graduated from Yale in 1766. Subsequently, he was admitted to the London bar from the Middle Temple in 1773.

Although Ingersoll's father was a Loyalist during the Revolution, the young man himself was an open supporter of the American cause. It is probable that his trip to the Continent in 1776 was really an attempt to remove himself from his father, and from any suspicion that he might be a partner in any of his father's pro-British activities.

Although Jared Ingersoll was one of Philadelphia's best known lawyers by the time of the Constitutional Convention, he was not very active in that body. He supported the document as it finally emerged, but he had played only a small part in its formulation.

As an attorney, however, Ingersoll was involved in some major cases, one of which posed a major threat to the Constitution in its early years. This was *Chisholm vs. Georgia*, in which Chisholm, the executor of an English property holder whose lands had been confiscated during the Revolution by Georgia, brought suit against that state to recover the appropriated land. Georgia refused to admit the right of Chisholm, a citizen of South Carolina, to bring suit against a state other than his own. Ingersoll, representing Georgia, lost the case before the Supreme Court, but eventually won when the Eleventh Amendment was passed, prohibiting precisely the type of legal action against which Ingersoll and his client had fought.

Perhaps even more interesting, at least in the context of the signers of the Constitution, is Ingersoll's defense of fellow signer William Blount in 1797. Blount had been expelled from the Senate for his involvement in a scheme to attack Spanish Florida and Louisiana. Blount was impeached by the House of Representatives, but he never came to trial before the Senate. Appar-

ently Ingersoll was skillful enough to avert a trial which might have ended Blount's career.

Jared Ingersoll never played a major role in national politics, though Pennsylvania Federalists urged his nomination for Vice-President in the election of 1812. He died in Philadelphia in 1822, just four days after his seventy-third birthday.

JAMES WILSON
Pennsylvania

September 14, 1742   *August 21, 1798*

James Wilson, who was born at Carskendo in the Scottish Lowlands, never lost either his native accent or his devotion to the study of law. After coming to America in 1765, he settled in Philadelphia. In 1774 he moved his law practice to Carlisle. By then, Wilson was growing increasingly involved in the assertion of American rights against what he saw as British oppression. It was during this year that Wilson wrote *Considerations on the Nature and Extent of the Legislative Authority of the British Parliament.* He distributed this pamphlet to all the delegates to the First Continental Congress. In this pamphlet, Wilson advocated immediate American independence.

Ironically, when the issue of independence actually came before the Second Continental Congress, Wilson could not quite bring himself to support it. He moved postponement of its consideration for a month, from June 8 to July 1. Wilson did vote for independence on July 2, 1776, but for the rest of his life became increasingly conservative in his political views. In fact, his conservative outlook provoked a mob assault on his Philadelphia home in 1779, a tight spot from which he was extricated by the local militia.

At the Constitutional Convention, Wilson was in his element. He and Madison were the two delegates most actively favoring a break from the Articles of Confederation, and their replacement with a more effective Constitution. Wilson served on the Committee of Detail which carefully arranged the Constitution, and he also strove energetically to win ratification of the new document by the Pennsylvania Convention. His efforts were successful, but the best he could do was win ratification on December 12, 1787, five days after Delaware had become the first of the Thirteen States to ratify.

Although James Wilson was appointed to the first United States Supreme Court by President Washington, this profound constitutional lawyer lived his last years under a cloud that grew increasingly dark. Unwisely committing many of his personal resources to investments in the opening Northwest Territory, Wilson came to grief. Weighed down by debts and hounded by creditors, he died in Edenton, North Carolina. As a Supreme Court Justice of that era, Wilson was traveling over his assigned circuit when death overtook him. His end seems unjust and tragic, and his passing cost the nation a valuable leader whose personal financial folly led to a discredited and tainted ending to a worthy and dedicated life.

GOUVERNEUR MORRIS
Pennsylvania
January 31, 1752   *November 6, 1816*

Gouverneur Morris was born in The Bronx, at Morrisania, his family estate, a younger half-brother of Lewis Morris, a signer of the Declaration of Independence. But Gouverneur Morris looms large in the story of the Federal Constitution not because of his birthplace or his relatives, but because of his exceptional skill with the pen. The Committee on Style of the Constitutional Convention entrusted the phrasing and expression of its ideas to Morris, knowing well that he would organize their points into a coherent and elegant document. Morris did so, adding his own distinct contribution in the Preamble, a succinct summing up of the national sense of purpose.

Gouverneur Morris, it is surprising to note, came to the Convention not as a delegate from New York but as one from Pennsylvania. The explanation is simple: he had left New York in a huff after suffering a political rebuff. But whatever state he came from, Morris talked enough at Philadelphia to make his presence keenly felt. He spoke intelligently, incisively, and interminably. His point of view was aristocratic, almost monarchic, but it was also national in scope. His was one of the most potent voices at Philadelphia for the creation of an American nation.

After the Convention, Morris served as Minister to France from 1792 to 1794, but became a victim of his own incautious support for Louis XVI and Marie Antoinette. The Jacobins in control of France's Revolutionary government eagerly sought a pretext for getting rid of him. In 1794 the reckless behavior of "Citizen" Genêt, whose arrogant disregard of courtesy and protocol made him *persona non grata* with President Washington, solved the Jacobins' problem. When Washington refused to receive Genêt's credentials, the French demanded Morris's recall.

Back in America, Gouverneur Morris plunged right into a swirl of activity. At first, he had to straighten out family business at Morrisania, but he soon returned to public affairs. From 1800 to 1803 he represented New York in the United States Senate. In 1810 he assumed the chair of the commission planning the

Erie Barge Canal. He also strongly denounced the Hartford Convention of 1815, an early threat to the integrity of the nation he had helped establish.

Probably the most astonishing event of his last years was Morris's marriage to Anne Carey Randolph on Christmas Day 1809. Anne was a sister of Thomas Mann Randolph, son-in-law of Thomas Jefferson. Her past had been clouded with charges of having brought about the death of her child born out of wedlock. Morris's reputation as a ladies' man had made him seem an unlikely candidate for marriage at the age of 57. Yet their few years together were happy. Anne's epitaph for her husband, buried at St. Ann's Episcopal Church in the South Bronx, called him "the best of men." If he was not altogether deserving of that superlative, he was certainly an outstanding patriot who had served his country with great distinction.

DELAWARE

GEORGE READ

Delaware

September 18, 1733   *September 21, 1798*

George Read was born in Maryland to an Irish father and a Welsh mother. Read was admitted to the Philadelphia bar in 1753, but moved to New Castle, Delaware, the following year. For the rest of his life, he practiced law in that medium-sized town.

This signer possessed several interesting distinctions. For one thing, he was one of the six signers of both the Declaration of Independence and the Constitution. This is especially noteworthy because Read had voted against independence on July 2, 1776, deciding to support the cause only barely in time to sign the document on August 2. Another notable distinction of Read's is that he was married to Gertrude Ross, sister of Pennsylvania Declaration signer, George Ross. More important than these two facets of Read's career, however, is the position he took at the

Federal Convention in Philadelphia. As a delegate from the small state of Delaware, Read shared the prevalent fear of large states like Massachusetts, Pennsylvania, and Virginia. But Read's idea of how to protect Delaware from its powerful neighbors differed from the ideas of other small states' men like William Paterson or fellow Delaware colleague Gunning Bedford, Jr. Read, like David Brearley, proposed abolishing existing state boundaries and redividing the total area and population into thirteen approximately equal regions. It is difficult to believe he was entirely serious about this, but he did indeed throw the Convention into consternation. Quixotic and futile as this plan appeared, it helped jolt both large and small states into a sense of reality. Read's idea significantly assisted in clearing the way for acceptance of the Connecticut Compromise, setting the number of representatives in the House and the Senate.

George Read was especially active at the Delaware ratification convention, and did much to assure that his state would be the first to assent to the new Federal Constitution.

After 1793, Read functioned almost exclusively in state government, notably as Chief Justice. He possessed an extensive personal library, filled with books annotated by him in all available margins.

Apparently George Read impressed different people in different ways. One historian called him tall and thin; William Pierce, in his notes, says Read was "of low stature." Pierce also complained that Read's "powers of Oratory are fatiguing and tiresome to the last degree; ... few can have the patience to attend to him." Nonetheless, this Founding Father was a distinguished contributor to the formulation, ratification, and early implementation of the Constitution which still animates our national existence.

GUNNING BEDFORD, JR.
Delaware
1749   *March 30, 1812*

One thing seems certain about Gunning Bedford: he was stout. William Pierce, who also described Bedford as "warm and impetuous in his temper, and precipitate in his judgment," concluded his sketch of Bedford by stating that he was "very corpulant [*sic*]."

Pierce's observations help us understand some of the extravagant statements Bedford made on the Convention floor. The most outrageous, undoubtedly, was his accusation that the large states were acting out of self-interest (as if the small states were not), but that this narrowmindedness by the populous states might drive the small states into forming alliances with foreign powers. Just to make sure that nobody from a large state could fail to feel offended, Bedford added officiously, "I do not, gentlemen, trust you."

As might have been expected, this outburst provoked an immediate protest, best expressed by Rufus King, who lamented that "the honorable gentleman from Delaware ... had declared himself ready to turn his hope from our common Country, and court the protection of some foreign land."

Though Bedford talked enough after this ill-considered barrage, his influence on his fellow delegates, understandably enough, was much reduced. It is perhaps surprising that a practicing lawyer should have proved so reckless in debate.

Bedford, a graduate of Princeton in 1771, had been a classmate of James Madison. Bedford had served in the Continental Congress, and been a delegate to the Annapolis Convention of 1786, an attempt to reach agreement concerning navigation of the Potomac River and Chesapeake Bay. Originally proposed by Virginia and Maryland, the Convention tried to draw a larger participation, but only five states actually attended. Surely he understood the urgent need for national unity implied in the Annapolis call to Congress for another convention, this time to meet in Philadelphia, to consider the state of government under the Articles of Confederation, and to propose remedies.

After the adjournment of the sessions in Philadelphia, Bedford returned to Delaware. He was a delegate to his state's ratifying convention, and also served as Delaware's Attorney General from 1784 to 1789. He had at first wanted only to amend the Articles of Confederation, but he subsequently endorsed the Constitution as it took its final form. He was an opponent of too powerful a central government and an advocate of a legislature unchecked by executive veto. It is quite possible that, even by the time he died in 1812, this Founding Father was not altogether certain just how satisfied he was with government under the Constitution he had helped to formulate and promote.

JOHN DICKINSON
Delaware

November 8, 1732   *February 14, 1808*

John Dickinson was active in the political lives of both Pennsylvania and Delaware, but the Pennsylvania commitment came first. It was there that Dickinson wrote *Letters from a Pennsylvania Farmer* during 1767 and 1768. These letters of protest against such British laws as the Stamp Act still packed political dynamite at the time of the break with England, earning Dickinson the sobriquet, "Penman of the Revolution." There is an irony in all this, for Dickinson feared the violent opposition to the Stamp Act even more than he disapproved of the act itself.

Dickinson clung to hope for reconciliation with England as long as he could. In 1775, after war had already broken out, the First Continental Congress drew up the "Olive Branch Petition" to King George III. Although Congress considered the petition futile, Dickinson got his way in making this one last attempt. The majority's judgment proved correct, but even a year later, when independence came up for a vote, Dickinson was not ready. With another reluctant patriot, Robert Morris, he absented himself from the session. Although at first unable to embrace independence, Dickinson quickly joined the cause once the national decision had been made. In short order, he buckled on his sword and entered military service. Few other members of Congress did that.

By 1779 Dickinson had made his move to Delaware and entered Congress from that state. At the convention of 1787, he was a frequent speaker and an ardent supporter of the Constitution as it began to take form. He urged it ahead in committee and in general session. This was especially important because some aspects of the Constitution, for example proportional representation in the House of Representatives, were not entirely to the taste of smaller states like Delaware. Dickinson's espousal of the Constitution helped nudge these states toward acceptance of the Connecticut Compromise. When the new national document came before the Delaware ratifying convention in December 1787, Dickinson was still pushing hard for it. He played no small role in gaining for Delaware the distinction of being the first state to ratify the national charter (December 7, 1787).

John Dickinson took little part in public life after 1787, although he lived until 1808. His last years were passed quietly near Dover, a locale he had known well as a boy. He first gained prominence in Pennsylvania, a large state, but his move to Delaware, a small state, was important in gaining support for the Constitution. Despite his early reluctance to declare for independence, John Dickinson, when he finally took his stand, played a leading role indeed in getting a new nation off on the right foot.

RICHARD BASSETT
Delaware

April 2, 1745   *September 15, 1815*

Richard Bassett was born the son of a tavernkeeper who later deserted his family. Consequently, Richard was adopted by an uncle, Peter Lawson, from whom he eventually inherited a substantial Maryland estate called Bohemia Manor.

During the Revolution, Bassett served as Captain of the Dover (Delaware) Light Horse. He spent ten years (1776-1786) in such positions as the Council of Safety, the State Constitutional Convention, and the State Legislature.

Although Bassett is nearly unknown today, he was a man of considerable repute during his lifetime. He should have possessed clear insights into the need for a strong national government, for he had been a delegate to the Annapolis Convention of 1786. But Bassett may have learned even more about governments and constitutions when he arrived in Philadelphia in May, 1787. While attending the Federal Convention sessions, he lodged at the Indian Queen Tavern. Among his fellow lodgers were Rutledge and Charles Pinckney of South Carolina, Williamson of North Carolina, Hamilton of New York, and Gorham of Massachusetts. One of the amenities provided for the delegates at this establishment was a hall or "common room," where they could meet in private, without endangering the Convention's rule of secrecy.

Despite all this exposure to Constitutional thought, however, Bassett made little noise at the Convention. Indeed, he seems to have impressed others more with his religious enthusiasm than with anything else. William Pierce described him as "a religious enthusiast, lately turned Methodist." The rest of Pierce's attitude toward Bassett stated that the Delaware delegate was "a Man of plain sense, and has modesty enough to hold his tongue."

It seems, however, there was more to Richard Bassett than Pierce discerned. This modest "religious enthusiast" served in the first United States Senate (1789-1793) and held the office of

Governor of Delaware (1799-1801). He may have been a modest man, but he was not an insignificant one.

Incidentally, you may remember from your history courses those "midnight judges" named by outgoing President John Adams in 1801 in an effort to hold at least the judiciary in Federalist hands. Bassett was one of these appointees.

JACOB BROOM
Delaware

1752   *April 25, 1810*

It may be somewhat unfair to refer to Jacob Broom as an ordinary man. The mere fact of his service at the Constitutional Convention indicates he must have been a cut or two above average. Perhaps we should describe him as one of those useful, reliable, but unheralded men who accomplish much while generating little noise or excitement.

We know very little about Broom. He was born in Wilmington, Delaware, served nearly a decade as a burgess of that town (1776-1785), was a founder of the Wilmington Library (1787), and served as Wilmington's first postmaster (1790-1792). Broom was an active promoter of manufacturing, earning his livelihood from the cotton mills he owned in northern Delaware. Unfortunately, there seems to be no authentic portrait of him in existence today. The picture we include here for completeness is surely not of him; both the whiskers and the clothing are of a later period. This illustration is probably that of one of his two sons who served in Congress.

William Pierce, who seems to have noticed Broom only in passing, described him as "silent in public," though "chearful [*sic*] and conversable in private." Yet Pierce seems to have failed to probe Broom quite deeply enough. On July 16, when the stand-off between large states and small states in the matter of representation threatened to dissolve the Convention, Broom urged the delegates to continue their deliberations. With good reason, he feared that collapse of the Convention could well mean failure to produce any sort of national government, and a continuing national disintegration. His plea succeeded, happily for the not-quite-formed United States.

After the Convention, Jacob Broom returned to Wilmington, where he devoted the rest of his life to his cotton mills and to civic affairs. It is of some interest that in 1802 he sold a piece of land on Brandywine Creek to E.I. du Pont. The cotton mill constructed there by Du Pont became the first outpost of the Du Pont industrial empire, still so powerful a component of Delaware's life and economy.

Broom died in Philadelphia, remembering in his will such charities as an organization to assist needy women and a school for black children. There was nothing brilliant about Jacob Broom; he was not one of the luminaries of his day. But he was a useful man whose life had its greatest impact on the local, rather than the national, scene.

MARYLAND

James McHenry

Dan of S Thos. Jenifer

Dan¹ Carroll

JAMES MCHENRY
Maryland

November 16, 1753   *May 3, 1816*

James McHenry was born in Northern Ireland, received a classical education in Dublin, and came to Philadelphia in 1771. He later moved to Baltimore where he inherited his father's merchandising establishment in 1790. Before settling into this phase of his life, McHenry had studied medicine under Dr. Benjamin Rush in Philadelphia, but his practice lasted only long enough to allow him to serve as a surgeon in the Continental Army, including a brief stint at Valley Forge.

Like James Madison, McHenry kept notes during the Constitutional Convention, which he attended briefly from May 28 to June 1, and to which he returned in August. Also like Madison, McHenry had been a member of Congress (1783-1786), and thus clearly perceived the need for a strong central government. No doubt this experience helped orient him politically toward the Federalist party, and prompted him to support the great document at the Maryland ratification convention.

In 1796, President Washington appointed McHenry Secretary of War. The Marylander proved a rather inept administrator; nonetheless, his tenure continued into the presidency of John Adams. The real problem with McHenry's cabinet service was not so much inefficiency as divided loyalty. Though serving under two Presidents, he looked to Alexander Hamilton as his actual leader, and gave his principal attention to the brilliant, if at times unscrupulous, New Yorker. Adams finally had enough of this, and demanded McHenry's resignation in 1800.

There is one irony in McHenry's life which is too good to omit even from a brief sketch. As was typical of the Federalists, McHenry was pro-British and opposed the War of 1812. But what is the one episode of that war known today to every

schoolchild? Surely it is Francis Scott Key's writing of "The Star Spangled Banner." The flag "was still there" over Fort McHenry, named for James when he was Secretary of War. Surely there is irony in the fact that the war's most memorable incident perpetuates the name of a Federalist ex-Secretary who detested the conflict and all it stood for.

DANIEL OF ST. THOMAS JENIFER
Maryland
1723   *November 16, 1790*

It is unfortunate that we do not know how Daniel of St. Thomas Jenifer got his middle name. It is so unusual that it must hold a story. The fascination increases when we learn that Jenifer had a brother whose name was simply Daniel, and that Daniel had two sons, one named Daniel and one named Daniel of St. Thomas. But, though we cannot account for the names, we do know that Jenifer was born in Charles County, Maryland, that he owned an estate called Stepney, and that he was exceptionally wealthy.

At 64, Jenifer was one of the oldest delegates to the Constitutional Convention, with considerable experience in public affairs by the time he reached Philadelphia in 1787. His years of service extended back to the last two Lords Proprietors of Maryland, continued through the Revolution, and on into the pre-Constitution Congress (1778-1782). His politics was conservative, favoring a permanent union of the states, hard money, and Congressional power to tax directly, rather than by levying requisitions on the states. Jenifer was thus in tune with the new Constitution right from the beginning. Both his experience and temperament made him an instant Federalist, and he continued his Federalism through the Maryland ratification convention.

This signer never married, and lived most of his adult life at Stepney. He was both an admirer and personal friend of George Washington, and a longtime, though generally inconspicuous, public servant.

Although Jenifer died in Annapolis, we do not today know where he is buried. It is possible that he may have been laid to rest in a Port Tobacco churchyard later washed out into the Potomac. Perhaps the fact that this bachelor had no descendants to look after such matters accounts for our ignorance of the site of his interment.

There is a little anecdote about Daniel of St. Thomas Jenifer that deals with his blustery fellow Maryland delegate at Philadelphia, Luther Martin. The latter was at that time a boisterous,

bellicose anti-Federalist who felt he could read the minds of the people of Maryland. At one time, within Jenifer's hearing, Martin vowed vociferously that he would be hanged if the people would support the Constitution. He was wrong, Maryland was the seventh state to ratify (April 26, 1788), and Jenifer's reply to the impudent boast proved sound advice. "Stay in Philadelphia," counseled Jenifer, "so the people of Maryland can't get to you with a length of rope."

DANIEL CARROLL
Maryland

July 22, 1730   *May 7, 1796*

Daniel Carroll belonged to the wealthy, powerful Catholic Carrolls of Maryland (there was also a Protestant branch of the family). Like many male Carrolls, including his cousin, Declaration signer Charles Carroll of Carrollton, young Daniel studied under English Jesuits in Flanders. So did Daniel's younger brother, John, who became the first American Catholic bishop.

Little is known of our delegate's early years. In 1781 he entered the Continental Congress and performed a task connected in no small way with the Federal Constitution. On March 1, Carroll signed the Articles of Confederation on behalf of Maryland. This state thus became the last of the thirteen to accept this agreement.

When Carroll came to Philadelphia in 1787, he was well

aware of the inadequacy of the existing government. By the time he had signed the Articles, their ineffectiveness already was evident. Consequently, Carroll was Federalist in his views, espousing a strong central government, and opposing the payment of Federal legislators' salaries by the states.

When the new government was formed, Carroll served in the First Congress (1789-1791). Before then, he had supported ratification at the Maryland convention.

Daniel Carroll played another role that had far more lasting consequences in terms of today's America. He was one of three commissioners charged with surveying and planning the District of Columbia. There were political enemies who contrived to make hay out of this arrangement, however. They pointed out that many of the lands being purchased for the Federal District belonged either to Daniel himself or to a nephew of the same name.

Finally, with Carroll, as with Daniel of St. Thomas Jenifer, the last resting place is unknown. Carroll died at Rock Creek, Maryland, but no record of his burial place has been found. It is a curious coincidence that two Founding Fathers from the same state, both named Daniel, should have passed into such posthumous anonymity.

Virginia

John Blair —
James Madison Jr

JOHN BLAIR
Virginia

1732   *August 31, 1800*

John Blair is one of those historical personages who should be well remembered but is not. Perhaps he just did not occupy the right places at the right times. Or maybe he was simply overshadowed by his two fellow signers from Virginia, George Washington and James Madison. And we must remember that the eighteenth century was so rich in great Virginians that John Blair could easily have appeared inconspicuous by comparison.

Blair was born in Williamsburg, Virginia, in the same year which saw Washington's birth. He attended William and Mary College, and later studied law at the Middle Temple in London (1755). As a resident of Williamsburg, Blair lived almost his entire life within walking distance of the functioning machinery of the Virginia government. He was a member of the House of

Burgesses (1766-1770), Clerk of the Governor's Council (1770-1775), a member of the Virginia state constitutional convention (1776), Judge of the General Court (1778), and Judge of Chancery (1780). John Blair brought to Philadelphia one of the most distinguished records of public service presented by any delegate. And yet he sat there at every session, completely silent. William Pierce noted this reticence on Blair's part, but put it into proper perspective. "Mr. Blair is ... no Orator, but his good sense and most excellent principles compensate for other deficiencies."

John Blair, however, impressed George Washington so much that he appointed this distinguished Virginia judge to a seat on the first United States Supreme Court. This could hardly have been a political repayment for Blair's silent support; it must, rather, have been a recognition of his good mind and his splendid legal background. It is also worth noting that another signer, James Wilson of Pennsylvania, also sat on that first Court, and that delegates William Paterson of New Jersey and Oliver Ellsworth of Connecticut were appointed during Washington's second term, the latter as Chief Justice. It might also be added that Justice Blair voted against the state of Georgia in *Chisholm vs. Georgia,* a case that involved Pennsylvania delegate Jared Ingersoll as counsel for Georgia, and which led ultimately to the adoption of the Eleventh Amendment.

John Blair died in Williamsburg, the town of his birth, in 1800. His house is still there, and he lies buried in Bruton churchyard, adjacent to the historic Episcopal church, at the edge of the restored area.

JAMES MADISON
Virginia

March 16, 1751   *June 28, 1836*

James Madison, although a Virginian, was a graduate of Princeton (1771). He traveled little, never saw Europe, and spent most of his life in his native state, yet he was never parochial in his outlook. He was governed by universal ideas and broad principles. He knew history, especially the political and legal history of the Western World, and, though small of stature, he thought big.

Just as stately George Washington contributed his imposing prestige to the Constitutional Convention, diminutive James Madison supplied ideas and knowledge. In an era when educated men were saturated with the history of Greece and Rome, Madison knew all that and classical law as well. Whether his intimate knowledge of the structure of ancient governments, as well as the causes of their failures, had much impact on his fellow delegates, or whether any significant number of classical ideas worked their way into the Federal Constitution is doubtful. But Madison had the ideas, and he knew how to adapt and modify them.

Although only 36 in 1787, Madison had much practical experience with government, and he came to Philadelphia as no solitary pedant or bookworm. He had seen the need for strong central rule; he had attended the Annapolis Convention of 1786, from which the call for a Philadelphia Convention emanated; and he had played a pivotal role in his state in disestablishing the Anglican Church, promoting commerce, and advocating improved transportation and communication. Freedom of religion, the advancement of human progress, and an appreciation of the need for cooperation were among the objectives Madison sought for the new Union. His knowledge of history, politics, and philosophy was the main tool he employed to attain these goals.

Madison's commitment to the Constitution did not end with the close of proceedings on September 17, 1787. He ardently supported the document as co-author of *The Federalist,* and he labored tirelessly to win ratification by his home state of Virginia.

During the Second Congress under the Constitution, Madison, then a member of the House of Representatives, shifted from the Federalists to the Antifederalists, the party of Thomas Jefferson. As Madison saw it, the Federal government, especially Alexander Hamilton and the Treasury Department, was becoming far too autocratic.

Madison's years as President (1809-1817) were difficult. It was the era of the Napoleonic Wars in Europe, and maritime America was caught between the two giants, England and France. The resulting War of 1812 caused him much grief because it generated serious disunity and uncovered national weakness.

We must not leave the "Father of the Constitution" without mentioning his wife, the legendary Dolley. Nor is it possible to neglect his lifelong friendship with Thomas Jefferson. If Jefferson shaped many of Madison's ideas and ideals, Dolley provided the sparkle her sometimes too serious husband occasionally needed.

The childless Madison, who had to endure a hell-raising son of Dolley's previous marriage, died a venerated national hero in 1836, the last of the Constitution's signers to pass away.

North Carolina

Wm Blount

Rich? Dobbs Spaight.

Hu Williamson

WILLIAM BLOUNT
North Carolina
March 26, 1749   *March 21, 1800*

William Blount's career took the form of an arch. He started at the bottom, went up one side during his promising early years, and came back down the other side at the end. While ascending the arch, Blount (pronounced blunt) in 1776 was paymaster for North Carolina troops. From 1781 to 1789 he served in the North Carolina legislature. In 1782-1783 and 1786-1787 he represented his state in Congress. Thus, when Blount attended at Philadelphia, he came from his Congressional duties in New York, and when the Convention had ended, Blount returned to his Congressional seat.

This signer continued his ascent by supporting the Constitution at North Carolina's second ratifying convention, in Fayetteville (1789), although he had signed the document reluctantly, intending his signature not so much as an indication of approval as an acquiescence that the Constitution was indeed a unanimous act of the states represented at the Convention.

Blount now entered a plateau period. Some things went well. In 1790 he was named Territorial Governor of Tennessee. In 1796 he presided over the convention that proclaimed Tennessee a state, and shortly thereafter, he was elected one of the state's first two Senators. But also in 1790, Blount began his disastrous and extravagant speculation in western lands. This speculation soon had Blount on the downside of his arch. He sank even deeper into debt, until he finally became receptive to the approaches of unscrupulous plotters. While the details remain obscure, we know that an incriminating letter was intercepted which implicated Blount in a half-mad plot to seize Spanish Florida and Louisiana with the help of Indians, frontiersmen, and the British. As a result, he was expelled from the United States Senate in July 1797 and impeached by the House of Representatives. Blount had slid to the bottom of his arch.

Yet he did rebound somewhat, being elected to the Tennessee state legislature in 1797. The Senate never convicted him, perhaps because of the legal exertions of Blount's counsel, fellow

Constitution signer Jared Ingersoll. In view of Blount's checkered career after his service at Philadelphia, the description of him by William Pierce seems ironic: "William Blount is a character strongly marked for integrity and honor ... he is plain, honest and sincere." Blount was apparently not quite so good as Pierce thought, but not quite so bad as he later seemed. This signer's home in Knoxville, Tennessee, can be visited today, and provides a reminder of him at his best, somewhere near the apex of his life's arch.

RICHARD DOBBS SPAIGHT
North Carolina
March 25, 1758   *September 6, 1802*

Dobbs is a famous name in North Carolina history; Richard Dobbs Spaight's mother was a sister of colonial Governor Arthur Dobbs. Despite this early advantage, however, Spaight had the misfortune to be orphaned at the age of eight. He was subsequently educated in Ireland, the country of his father's people, and completed his studies in Scotland at the University of Glasgow.

This sort of background would seem to have indicated Loyalist leanings and the advisability of remaining in Great Britain until the Revolution had ended. Nevertheless, Spaight returned to North Carolina in 1778, and in 1779 was elected to the North Carolina House of Commons from New Bern. This did not prevent him from seeing military service, especially at the disastrous Battle of Camden (South Carolina) in 1780. By war's end, Spaight had attained the rank of Lieutenant-Colonel of artillery.

From 1781 to 1787 Spaight served in the North Carolina House of Commons, being its Speaker in 1785. At the Constitutional Convention in Philadelphia he advocated seven-year terms for the President and the Senators, and the election of Senators by the state legislatures. Only the last recommendation found its way into the Constitution, though it was repealed in 1913 by the Seventeenth Amendment. Spaight played only a minor role in effecting North Carolina's eventual ratification of the Constitution.

This signer served three one-year terms as Governor of North Carolina (1792-1795), and was a presidential elector in 1793. From 1798 to 1801 he served in Congress, favoring repeal of the Alien and Sedition Laws, and generally adhering to the politics of Jefferson and Madison. During his last two years in Congress, Spaight claimed that ill health made his attendance irregular, and that assertion led to his life's ultimate tragedy.

In 1802, Federalist John Stanly of New Bern, North Carolina, was elected to Spaight's Congressional seat. Unfortunately, Stanly had accused Spaight of using his illness as an excuse to avoid

controversial votes in Congress. Understandably, Spaight resented the charge, and replied with a handbill vilifying Stanly. The latter issued a challenge to the September 5 duel that resulted in Spaight's fatal wounding. Although Stanly was charged with murder, he was later pardoned by North Carolina Governor James Turner.

HUGH WILLIAMSON
North Carolina

December 5, 1735   *May 22, 1819*

Hugh Williamson is unquestionably one of the most interesting signers of the Federal Constitution. He was born in Pennsylvania and died in New York City. He was educated at the College of Philadelphia (now the University of Pennsylvania), and had originally intended to enter the Presbyterian ministry. However, the doctrinal division of that period between the Old Lights and the New Lights deflected him from his original purpose and turned him toward medicine. He went to Europe and obtained his M.D. from the University of Utrecht in the Netherlands.

Williamson subsequently combined a rather modest medical practice with a vigorous business career in Edenton, North Carolina, a port once thought to hold great commercial promise, but which is now a quiet little coastal town.

Throughout his life, Williamson was recognized as a scholar and a man of learning. In 1768 he was elected to the American Philosophical Society in Philadelphia. In the following year, that Society named him to a commission to study the transits of Venus and Mercury across the face of the sun. Also in 1769, Williamson proposed a theory that every planet and comet was inhabited by living things. He would win no prizes for his theory today, but we must remember that in 1769 knowledge of the universe was comparatively primitive, and his means of studying the planets and stars were utterly inadequate. But this signer was well informed by the scientific standards of his day, and carried on an extensive correspondence with other scientists, especially Benjamin Franklin.

Hugh Williamson came to Philadelphia in 1787 as an experienced participant in government. He had served in the North Carolina House of Commons and in the Continental Congress (1782-1785). At the Convention he favored a strong central government, as most businessmen did. Only when the ardent states' rights advocate Willie Jones refused to attend the Convention was Williamson named, but he was by far the most active North Carolina delegate in Philadelphia. He argued forcefully for the Great Compromise, and played a major role in its ultimate adoption.

Williamson was not a delegate to the Hillsborough ratification convention of 1788. Perhaps that is one reason ratification failed at that time. But in 1789, at Fayetteville, Williamson was present and North Carolina ratified.

The last years of Williamson's life were spent in New York City, where, among other achievements, he served as one of the state's Congressmen. After 1793 his interests centered on the New York Hospital, the City Dispensary, the Humane Society, and the New-York Historical Society. When he died in 1819, Hugh Williamson left behind an enviable record of public service and generous philanthropy. He is buried in Trinity Churchyard at Wall Street, but you will find no tombstone for him. He is with the Apthorps, his wife's family, and no special mention of his interment is made on the Apthorp vault.

SOUTH CAROLINA

JOHN RUTLEDGE
South Carolina

September 1739   *July 18, 1800*

John Rutledge knew his way around in governmental matters. Educated in England, as were all South Carolina's signers, Rutledge had served in his colony's House of Commons and been prominent in opposing the Stamp Act (1765). He was a member of the First Continental Congress (1774). He served on a committee to draw up South Carolina's original state Constitution (1776). He twice held the office of governor during the Revolution, and distinguished himself by his tireless efforts to maintain support for the American cause, especially after Gates's defeat at Camden (South Carolina). In this work, Rutledge provided ardent support for Generals Nathanael Greene and Francis Marion during their Southern campaigns.

At the Constitutional Convention, Rutledge was impressively active and influential. He chaired the Committee of Detail, which organized the Convention's resolutions into a coherent form. He was a member of the Committee on Representation, which submitted the Great Compromise on representation in the Senate and the House of Representatives. He fought to prevent dissolution of the Convention when that misfortune seemed imminent. It might be added here too that John Rutledge's younger brother Edward was a signer of the Declaration of Independence and also a Governor of South Carolina.

Tragedy began to stalk John Rutledge in 1792, however. In that year his wife died, and he began to show signs of increasing mental instability. Furthermore, in 1795, the signing of the Federalist-backed Jay Treaty with England evoked Rutledge's vociferous disapproval. He believed that the treaty bartered the interests of the South and West for the advantage of the commercial Northeast. Consequently, when Washington named Rutledge Chief Justice of the United States (1795), the Senate, under Federalist control, refused to confirm the appointment. To replace Rutledge, Washington named Oliver Ellsworth of Connecticut, a delegate to the Constitutional Convention, though not one of the signers.

Perhaps it is just as well that Rutledge's nomination was rejected. His mental condition continued to deteriorate until his death in 1800, and he would surely have been incapable of serving long as Chief Justice. Yet his rejection resulted from political vindictiveness rather than any sympathetic compassion for his misfortune. This distinguished leader deserved a kinder fate.

CHARLES COTESWORTH PINCKNEY
South Carolina
February 25, 1746   *August 16, 1825*

Charles Cotesworth Pinckney is not to be confused with his second cousin, Charles Pinckney. For one thing, Charles Cotesworth was eleven years older. Furthermore, he played the cello, a talent just plain Charles lacked.

Charles Cotesworth's father was appointed South Carolina's colonial agent in London in 1753. The whole family therefore moved to England, including Pinckney's remarkable mother, Elizabeth (Lucas), who played a major role in introducing the cultivation of the dye-producing plant indigo into her colony.

Young Pinckney studied at Oxford and the Middle Temple law school. He was admitted to the English bar in 1769, but returned to South Carolina later that year, setting up practice in his native colony.

South Carolina's powerful families were often tightly interconnected by marriage, and Pinckney fitted into this characteristic pattern. He married the sister of Arthur Middleton, a South Carolina signer of the Declaration of Independence.

Pinckney served in the South Carolina Provincial Assembly (1769), in the Provincial Congress (1775), and in the State Senate (1779). During the Revolution he acted as aide-de-camp to Washington at the Battles of Brandywine and Germantown. He commanded a regiment at Savannah when it fell in 1778. He escaped then, but was captured two years later at the fall of Charleston.

By the time Pinckney reached the Constitutional Convention, he had already led a full life as a lawyer, statesman, and soldier. He was active throughout the sessions, serving on the Committee on Trade and Navigation at Philadelphia, and strongly supporting the Constitution at South Carolina's ratifying convention in 1788. In the latter case, the weaving of family ties into South Carolina politics proved especially advantageous. The convention was presided over by Charles Cotesworth's brother, Governor Thomas Pinckney.

In later years Pinckney seemed willing to run for public office only when he had little chance of winning. Outright appoint-

ments he usually declined, although in 1797 he did serve with Elbridge Gerry and John Marshall in the XYZ Affair with France, in which three French diplomats (X, Y, and Z) demanded bribes from the American envoys to negotiate an end to raids on American shipping. Pinckney and his two colleagues refused to comply. In 1795 Pinckney declined appointment as Secretary of State, and in 1804 and 1808 he ran as a Federalist Presidential candidate, elections he was in no danger of winning, for his party was in decline and his opponents were, successively, Jefferson and Madison.

When Pinckney died in 1825, only three other signers of the Constitution still survived, Rufus King, William Few, and James Madison. This outstanding South Carolinian had lived one of the most interesting, diversified and distinguished lives of any of his contemporaries.

CHARLES PINCKNEY
South Carolina
October 26, 1757   *October 29, 1824*

Charles Pinckney, cousin of Charles Cotesworth Pinckney, had a youthful appearance which gave little hint of the political experience he brought to the Constitutional Convention. William Pierce described him as "only 24 yrs. of age," though Pinckney was in fact nearly thirty. But Pierce did not miss Pinckney's endowments. He was "in possession of a very great variety of knowledge — Government, Law, History and Phylosophy [*sic*] are his favorite studies, but he is intimately acquainted with every species of polite learning, and has a spirit of application and industry beyond most men."

Like all the South Carolina signers, Pinckney had studied in England. But in his case the time had been short, for he was admitted to the Middle Temple in 1773, but was back in South Carolina by 1775. In 1780, Pinckney was among the 5,000 Americans surrendered at Charleston by General Benjamin Lincoln.

At the Convention Pinckney presented an alternate governmental plan that was, however, never discussed in actual debate. The delegates worked almost exclusively on the plan proposed by Edmund Randolph on behalf of the Virginia delegation. Pinckney, of course, defended Southern interests at Philadelphia, especially with respect to the slave trade, basis of representation, and commerce. He heartily endorsed the Constitution as it finally evolved, and backed its acceptance at the South Carolina ratification convention in the spring of 1788.

Pinckney's later years were rich in public service. He served as Federalist Governor of South Carolina (1789-1792). But his vehement reaction to the Jay Treaty of 1795 led to his alienation from his Federalist colleagues. Gradually he drifted into the Jeffersonian orbit, and was twice elected Governor as a Democrat-Republican (1796-1798, 1806-1808). In between (1801) Jefferson appointed him Minister to Spain. A notable achievement of this period was the restoration to Americans of the right of deposit at New Orleans, the right to deliver goods there for transshipment and export. After the Louisiana Purchase (1803), Pinckney

tried to induce Spain to cede Florida to the United States. He was unsuccessful, however, and returned to South Carolina in 1805. From 1819 to 1821, he served in Congress, although reluctantly. During his term the Missouri Compromise (1820) came before Congress, a measure he vigorously but vainly opposed.

Charles Pinckney closed his life and career in 1824, one of the last of the Philadelphia signers to die. His change from Federalist to Jeffersonian politics earned him the disdain of his former political allies, and the opprobrious nickname "Blackguard Charlie." But he had served his state and his country with great ability and dedication.

PIERCE BUTLER
South Carolina
July 11, 1744   *February 15, 1822*

Irish-born Pierce Butler was a professional soldier, assigned to America, who liked the country so much that he resigned his commission and settled in South Carolina (1773). He married well (Mary Middleton in 1771), and the alliance with her family opened numerous political and commercial doors in South Carolina.

Butler served in the state legislature (1778-1782, 1784-1789), but took a political stance quite different from that of his fellow plantation owners. He tended to be a populist, championing what he saw as the cause of the poor, back-country farmers. This attitude was probably partly due to personal conviction, and partly to his dislike of some of the other plantation owners.

One concrete result of Butler's political activity was the moving of the state capital from Charleston to Columbia in 1790.

At the Constitutional Convention, Butler favored a strong central government, but he was notably sensitive to any encroachments on Southern rights with respect to either slavery or international commerce. He was the author of the fugitive slave clause of the Constitution, and defended the new Federal Constitution before its South Carolina critics, although he was not himself a delegate to the ratification convention.

When the new national government went into effect in 1789, Butler was one of the state's first Senators. He remained in the Senate until 1796, and from 1802 to 1804 he sat in the Senate again, resigning in dismay after the adoption of the Twelfth Amendment, which provided for separate election of President and Vice-President, rather than the original provision that gave the Presidency to the candidate with the most votes and the Vice-Presidency to the runner-up.

Pierce Butler lived his last years in Philadelphia, disappointed that he had no sons. To try to compensate somewhat for this lack, he persuaded a son-in-law to name his oldest son Pierce Butler in order that he might inherit Butler's South Carolina plantation.

This grandson was indeed so named, but he was rash enough to marry the English actress Fanny Kemble. In 1834 Fanny moved into her plantation home, but was so horrified by the slavery she observed that she quickly wanted out. She obtained a divorce and described her traumatic experiences in *Journal of a Residence in America.*

GEORGIA

William Few

Abr Baldwin

WILLIAM FEW
Georgia

June 8, 1748   *July 16, 1828*

All three of Georgia's signers of the Declaration of Independence and both that state's signers of the Constitution came from other, often distant, places. Georgia was small and growing during the late eighteenth century, an attractive area to up-and-coming leaders and aspiring professionals; attractive, that is, if the newcomer was not unduly troubled by slavery.

William Few was born in Maryland, but in 1758 moved with his family to North Carolina. The Fews were not wealthy, and William grew up surrounded by the challenges of frontier life, a condition brought forcefully home to him in 1771 during the uprising of the Regulators in North Carolina. This group, rebelling against what they considered excessive and unreasonable taxation by the aristocracy, challenged the public authorities under Governor William Tryon (later colonial Governor of New York; that city's Fort Tryon Park is named for him). The colonial forces soundly defeated the Regulators at the Battle of the Alamance. Few's brother James was captured at the battle and hanged as a rebel. Understandably, the Fews felt it desirable to move again, this time to Georgia.

During the Revolution, Few served as a Lieutenant-Colonel of Georgia militia. He was twice a member of the Georgia General Assembly, and in 1783 he represented his state in Congress. At the Constitutional Convention in 1787, Few was one of the two Georgia delegates (out of four) who remained until the end and signed the document. His fellow Georgia delegate, William Pierce, had little to say about Few except that he "possesses a strong natural Genius, and from application has acquired some knowledge of legal matters; — he practices at the bar of Georgia, and speaks tolerably well in the Legislature."

In the new Federal government, Few served as one of Georgia's first two Senators. In 1796 he was named judge in the Second Federal District of Georgia. However, in 1799, Few moved to New York and soon established himself in that state, winning election to its Assembly, appointment as inspector of state prisons,

and a chair among the aldermen of New York City.

The rest of Few's life was passed in New York, where for ten years (1804-1814) he was a director of the Manhattan Bank. He was also serving as President of the City Bank at the close of his business career. Few spent his last years living with a daughter and her family at Fishkill Landing (now Beacon), New York. Why had he come to New York after so successful a career in Georgia? The most commonly advanced explanation is his aversion to slavery. Georgia was not then so attractive a state to one who held that practice in abhorrence.

ABRAHAM BALDWIN
Georgia
November 22, 1754   *March 4, 1807*

Abraham Baldwin was a native of North Guilford, Connecticut, who followed the path of opportunity south to Georgia. But that came later. In 1775, Baldwin's father, a blacksmith, moved his family to New Haven in order that his children might have adequate educational opportunities. The move did not affect Abraham much; he had already graduated from Yale, but the relocation did involve him in the care and training of his younger brothers and sisters.

In 1775 Baldwin was licensed as a minister, and for the next four years he tutored at Yale. In 1779 he held a chaplaincy in the Revolutionary Army. In 1781, he was offered a chair of divinity at Yale, but declined. After this year, he left the ministry, studied law, and was admitted to the bar in 1783. To further himself in this profession, he left Connecticut in 1784 and settled in Georgia.

It did not take Baldwin long to make his mark in his adopted state. In 1785 he was elected to the State Assembly. At the same time, he was deeply involved in helping establish the University of Georgia.

At the Constitutional Convention Baldwin was understandably much influenced by the Connecticut delegation, especially with regard to the Great Compromise, which he had, at first, opposed. In fact, he served on the Grand Committee which presented this compromise to the Convention.

Baldwin served in the First Congress, and retained his seat in the House of Representatives for ten years (1789-1799). From 1799 to 1807 he served in the Senate, an opponent of the fiscal policies of Alexander Hamilton, an objector to the Jay Treaty of 1795, and a protestor against the Alien and Sedition Laws of 1798. He supported the policies of Thomas Jefferson, and voted for the conviction of Supreme Court Justice Samuel Chase on three of the eight counts against him in his impeachment trial (1804). Baldwin's sister Ruth, it might be mentioned, married

the New England literary figure, Joel Barlow, an old college chum of her brother at Yale.

Apparently, Baldwin did not have the same problem with slavery that William Few did. Baldwin consistently defended the South's interest in its "peculiar institution." He died in Washington, D.C., in 1807, and is buried there in Rock Creek Cemetery.

THE NONSIGNING DELEGATES

Of the fifty-five delegates who attended the Consitutional Convention at one time or other, sixteen failed to sign the final document. Some of the nonsigners were opposed to the Constitution as it finally emerged; others approved the new national charter, but were unable for personal reasons to be present at the time of the signing. Below are listed the delegates who did not sign, with a note in each case to explain why the individual did not affix his signature to the Federal Constitution.

Massachusetts

Elbridge Gerry believed that the people would reject the Constitution as written, and that ratification, if it came about, would lead to civil war. Gerry later became Governor of Massachusetts and Vice-President of the United States in Madison's second term. While governor, Gerry attempted a redistricting of his state to favor the future election of members of his Democratic-Republican party. This effort has enriched our language with the word "gerrymander." Gerry died as Vice-President of the United States in 1814.

Caleb Strong favored the Constitution and supported its ratification at the Massachusetts convention. He left Philadelphia before he could sign because of illness in his family. In 1789 he was elected Senator from Massachusetts, and in 1800 he defeated Elbridge Gerry to become governor of his state. He opposed the War of 1812, and supported the secessionist Hartford Convention of 1815. Strong died at Northampton, Massachusetts, in 1819.

Connecticut

Oliver Ellsworth supported the Constitution, and defended it at the Connecticut ratifying convention. "Pressing domestic considerations," as he put it, forced him to leave Philadelphia before he could sign. In 1796, President Washington appointed Ellsworth Chief Justice of the United States. He died in 1807 at his home in Windsor, Connecticut.

New York

John Lansing, Jr. and **Robert Yates** both left Philadelphia on July 10. They were under instruction not to go beyond revising the Articles of Confederation. They left the Convention when it became clear that the delegates would go well beyond mere revision. Both opposed ratification at the New York convention. Lansing served as a New York State judge from 1790 to 1801. From 1801 to 1814 he was Chancellor of the state. On the evening of December 12, 1829, Lansing left his hotel to mail some letters on the Albany boat, docked at the foot of Cortlandt Street. He was never seen or heard from again.

Robert Yates served as Associate and later Chief Justice of New York from 1792 to 1798. In 1800 he was named to a commission to settle Indian land claims in Onondaga County. He died in 1801, and twenty years later his widow published his notes taken during his stay at the Constitutional Convention.

New Jersey

William Churchill Houston was extremely ill at the time of the Convention, and took little part in it. He died less than a year later of tuberculosis.

Maryland

John Francis Mercer and **Luther Martin** both opposed the Constitution as insufficiently democratic, especially in its lack of a bill of rights. They both opposed ratification at the Maryland convention. Luther Martin had married Maria Cresap in 1783. In his *Notes on Virginia*, Thomas Jefferson accused Michael Cresap, Maria's father, of the murder of the Indian chief, Logan. Martin attacked Jefferson in a series of published letters to which Jefferson refused to reply. The ensuing antagonism drove Martin, of all people, into the Federalist party. His life was unhappy, plagued by the early death of his wife, the insanity of a daughter, and his own uncontrolled alcoholism. He died at the home of Aaron Burr in New York City in 1826.

John Francis Mercer later served in the House of Representatives (1791 to 1794) after two terms in the Maryland House of Delegates. He died in 1821, after having fathered 19 children in two marriages.

Virginia

Edmund Randolph vacillated, stating that he refused to sign because he feared the people would reject the Constitution, and chaos would result. Randolph may, in fact, have feared that Virginia would reject the Constitution, compromising his political future there if he supported it. However, at his state's convention, he reversed himself, and advocated ratification. Randolph later held two positions in Washington's cabinet, Attorney General and Secretary of State. In 1795, rumors that Randolph was involved in improper dealings with a French diplomat led to the Secretary's resignation. Randolph denied any wrongdoing, returned to his law practice, and wrote a history of Virginia. He died in 1813.

George Mason strongly distrusted any powerful central government as destructive of the liberties won by the Revolution. He thus opposed the Constitution and fought its ratification at Richmond. Subsequently, Mason retired to his estate, Gunston Hall, and took no further part in public life. He died in 1792, a revered friend of three other great Virginians: George Washington, Thomas Jefferson, and James Madison.

George Wythe favored the Constitution, and supported it in the Virginia ratifying convention. He left Philadelphia early only because of his wife's illness. At William and Mary College Wythe became the first professor of law in the United States (1779 to 1790), and from 1788 to 1801 he served as Chancellor of Virginia. Wythe died tragically in 1806, almost certainly poisoned by a grandnephew impatient to get at his share of Wythe's estate. Before his death, which was protracted and painful, Wythe disinherited the grandnephew, but the latter was never convicted, for the chief witness against him was Wythe's black cook, whose testimony at that time could not be used against a white.

James McClurg left the Convention early, but is believed to have favored the Constitution. Little is known about why he did not sign or why he left so prematurely. He was, however, a political novice who felt himself lost during the discussions. After leaving the Convention, McClurg returned to his practice of medicine at Richmond.

North Carolina

Alexander Martin left Philadelphia in August, lacking enthusiasm for the Constitution, though he later supported it at the second North Carolina ratifying convention, at Fayetteville, in 1789. Martin served as governor of his state from 1789 to 1792, and in the latter year went to the United States Senate. At the end of his Senate term, he returned to his plantation and held only state offices after that. He never married, and died on his plantation in 1807.

William Richardson Davie went home early because of family illness. He defended the Constitution at the Fayetteville state convention in 1789. In later years he became a founder of the University of North Carolina, and governor in 1798. He denounced the Kentucky and Virginia Resolutions that threatened the Federal union before it had lived a decade. He was a Federalist who deeply distrusted Thomas Jefferson and his politics. He opposed the War of 1812, though remaining on cordial personal terms with James Madison. Davie died in 1820.

Georgia

William Pierce, best known for his thumbnail sketches of his fellow delegates, returned to Georgia early to attend to some serious business setbacks. He died in 1789, only two years after the Convention, and just a few months into the life of the new national government. In 1828 Pierce's notes of the Convention were published in Savannah.

William Houstoun opposed the eligibility of the President for re-election, and favored only a revision of the Articles of Confederation. He returned to Congress after his brief attendance, but little is known of his subsequent life. He is not even mentioned in the *Dictionary of American Biography.*

COMMITTEE MEMBERSHIP

Committee of the Whole.

This committee consisted of the entire membership of the Constitutional Convention. Its purpose was to enable the members to debate and vote informally, without following the usual parliamentary rules, and without being committed to any position. No votes were recorded, making it easier to thrash out controversial topics without taking a definitive stand.

Nathaniel Gorham (Massachusetts), Chairman

Committee on Rules.

This committee formulated the formal rules which would govern the proceedings of the Convention. The most debated and best known of these rules was the rule of secrecy that bound every delegate concerning the content of the discussions.

George Wythe (Virginia), Chairman
Alexander Hamilton (New York) and Charles Pinckney (South Carolina)

Grand Committee on Trade and Navigation.

The principal contribution of this committee was its proposal to limit the rate of taxation on slaves, and a recommendation that the slave trade be prohibited after 1800. The Convention eventually adopted 1808 as the cut-off time for slave importation. The committee also suggested a ban on interstate tariffs.

William Livingston (New Jersey), Chairman
John Langdon (New Hampshire), Rufus King (Massachusetts), William Samuel Johnson (Connecticut), George Clymer (Pennsylvania), John Dickinson (Delaware), Luther Martin (Maryland), James Madison (Virginia), Hugh Williamson (North Carolina), Charles Cotesworth Pinckney (South Carolina), Abraham Baldwin (Georgia).

Grand Committee on Representation.

This committee presented a recommendation that representation in the House be according to population, and in the Senate equal for each state.

Elbridge Gerry (Massachusetts), Chairman
Oliver Ellsworth (Connecticut), Robert Yates (New York),
William Paterson (New Jersey), Benjamin Franklin
(Pennsylvania), Gunning Bedford (Delaware),
Luther Martin (Maryland), George Mason (Virginia),
William Richardson Davie (North Carolina),
John Rutledge (South Carolina), Abraham Baldwin
(Georgia).

Committee of Detail.

This committee was asked to organize all the propositions
and resolutions debated up until that time, to arrange them
in systematic fashion, and to present them for debate as a
coherent, unified document. While this committee tackled its
assignment, the rest of the delegates enjoyed the Fourth of
July holiday.

John Rutledge (South Carolina), Chairman
Edmund Randolph (Virginia), James Wilson
(Pennsylvania), Nathaniel Gorham (Massachusetts),
Oliver Ellsworth (Connecticut).

Committee on Style.

This committee wrote the Constitution in the form we know
today. The actual writing was done by Gouverneur Morris,
though the rest of the committee reviewed and approved
what Morris had written.

William Samuel Johnson (Connecticut), Chairman
Alexander Hamilton (New York), Gouverneur Morris
(Pennsylvania), James Madison (Virginia),
Rufus King (Massachusetts).

A grand committee was one composed of one delegate from
each of the states. In the case of these committees, the number
of members was usually eleven. The reason is simply that Rhode
Island never sent any delegates to the Convention, and either the
two delegates from New Hampshire arrived after the committee
had been formed, or the New York delegates had left before the
committee had been constituted. In the case of the Grand Committee on Trade and Navigation, New Hampshire was represented (Langdon), but the New York delegates had already left.
In the case of the Grand Committee on Representation, the New
York delegates were represented, but the New Hampshire delegates had not yet arrived.

ALPHABETICAL LIST OF THE SIGNERS OF THE FEDERAL CONSTITUTION

Abraham Baldwin	Georgia
Richard Bassett	Delaware
Gunning Bedford, Jr.	Delaware
John Blair	Virginia
William Blount	North Carolina
David Brearley	New Jersey
Jacob Broom	Delaware
Pierce Butler	South Carolina
Daniel Carroll	Maryland
George Clymer	Pennsylvania
Jonathan Dayton	New Jersey
John Dickinson	Delaware
William Few	Georgia
Thomas FitzSimons	Pennsylvania
Benjamin Franklin	Pennsylvania
Nicholas Gilman	New Hampshire
Nathaniel Gorham	Massachusetts
Alexander Hamilton	New York
Jared Ingersoll	Pennsylvania
Daniel of St. Thomas Jenifer	Maryland
William Samuel Johnson	Connecticut
Rufus King	Massachusetts
John Langdon	New Hampshire
William Livingston	New Jersey
James Madison	Virginia
James McHenry	Maryland
Thomas Mifflin	Pennsylvania
Gouverneur Morris	Pennsylvania
Robert Morris	Pennsylvania
William Paterson	New Jersey
Charles Pinckney	South Carolina
Charles Cotesworth Pinckney	South Carolina
George Read	Delaware
John Rutledge	South Carolina
Roger Sherman	Connecticut
Richard Dobbs Spaight	North Carolina
George Washington	Virginia
Hugh Williamson	North Carolina
James Wilson	Pennsylvania

THE RATIFICATION OF
THE CONSTITUTION BY STATES

State	Date of Ratification	Vote
Delaware	December 7, 1787	unanimous
Pennsylvania	December 12, 1787	46-23
New Jersey	December 18, 1787	unanimous
Georgia	January 2, 1788	unanimous
Connecticut	January 9, 1788	128-40
Massachusetts	February 6, 1788	187-168
Maryland	April 26, 1788	63-11
South Carolina	May 23, 1788	149-73
New Hampshire *	June 21, 1788	57-47
Virginia	June 25, 1788	89-79
New York	July 26, 1788	30-27
North Carolina #	November 21, 1789	195-77
Rhode Island	May 29, 1790	34-32

* *With New Hampshire's ratification, the ninth state to do so, the Constitution went into effect for the states that had ratified. As the other states subsequently ratified, they, in fact, joined a union that already existed.*

North Carolina had at first rejected the Constitution at the Hillsborough convention in 1788; the state ratified at its second convention in Fayetteville.

BIBLIOGRAPHY

Below are listed several books that may be of interest to readers of these biographical sketches. All of the principal delegates to the Constitutional Convention have been the subject of biographies, and several of the signers have been studied many times by many authors. I have not attempted to include biographies in this listing because they would be too numerous for the space allotted. The works listed are ones which relate to the Constitution itself, the Convention, or to the ratification process.

Bowen, Catherine Drinker. *Miracle at Philadelphia.* Little, Brown (1966).

Butzner, Jane. *Constitutional Chaff.* Columbia University Press (1941).

Elliot, Jonathan. *Debates in the Several State Conventions on the Adoption of the Federal Constitution.* 5 vols. (1901).

Farrand, Max. *The Framing of the Constitution of the United States.* Yale University Press (1913).

Farrand, Max. *The Records of the Federal Convention of 1787.* 4 Vols. Yale University Press (1937).

Koch, Adrienne (ed.). *Notes of Debates in the Federal Convention of 1787, Reported by James Madison.* Ohio University Press (1965).

McLaughlin, Andrew C. *The Confederation and the Constitution.* Reprint of 1905 original. Collier Books (1962).

Padover, Saul. *The Living United States Constitution.* Mentor Books (1953).

Rossiter, Clinton (ed.). *The Federalist.* New American Library (1961). There are many other editions of *The Federalist,* but of special interest to Bronxites is the 1863 edition by Henry B. Dawson, published by Scribner. Dawson was a resident of The Bronx.

Rutland, R.A. *The Ordeal of the Constitution.* University of Oklahoma Press (1966).

Van Doren, Carl. *The Great Rehearsal.* Viking Press (1948).

Warren, Charles. *The Making of the Constitution.* Harvard University Press (1928).

Whitney, David C. *Founders of Freedom in America,* Vol. II. J.G. Ferguson (1965).

PUBLICATIONS OF
THE BRONX COUNTY HISTORICAL SOCIETY

The Beautiful Bronx (1920-1950) by Lloyd Ultan
The Bronx in the Innocent Years (1890-1925) by Lloyd Ultan
    and Gary Hermalyn
*The Bronx in Print: An Annotated Catalogue of Books and
    Pamphlets about The Bronx* edited by Candace Kuhta
    and Narcisco Rodriguez
The Bronx Triangle: A Portrait of Norwood by Edna Mead
*Genealogy of The Bronx: An Annotated Guide to Sources of
    Information* by Gary Hermalyn, Janet Butler and Laura Tosi
History in Asphalt: The Origin of Bronx Street and Place Names
    by John McNamara
History of the Morris Park Racecourse and the Morris Family
    by Nicholas Di Brino
Legacy of The Revolution: The Valentine-Varian House by
    Lloyd Ultan
*Morris High School and the Creation of the New York City
    Public High School System* by Gary Hermalyn
Edgar Allan Poe: A Short Biography by Kathleen A. McAuley
Poems of Edgar Allan Poe at Fordham edited by Elizabeth Beirne
The Signers of the Constitution of the United States by
    Brother C. Edward Quinn

Periodicals

The Bronx County Historical Society Journal
*The Bronx Historian: Newsletter of The Bronx County
    Historical Society*
Eureka: Newsletter of the Friends of Edgar Allan Poe Cottage
*Library News: Newsletter of The Bronx County Historical
    Society Library*

VALENTINE-VARIAN HOUSE

c. 1758

MUSEUM OF BRONX HISTORY

The Valentine-Varian House, owned and administered by
The Bronx County Historical Society,
was donated by Mr. William C. Beller.

3266 Bainbridge Avenue at East 208th Street
Telephone: (212) 881-8900

◆

The Bronx County Historical Society is supported
in part with public funds and services provided through
The Department of Cultural Affairs and
The Department of Parks and Recreation of The City of New York,
The Office of the President of the Borough of The Bronx,
New York State Office of Parks, Recreation and Historic Preservation,
and the Institute of Museum Services

THE BRONX COUNTY HISTORICAL SOCIETY

The Bronx County Historical Society was founded in 1955 for the purpose of promoting knowledge, interest and research in The Bronx. The Society administers The Museum of Bronx History, Edgar Allan Poe Cottage, a Research Library, and The Bronx County Archives; publishes a varied series of books, journals and newsletters; conducts historical tours, lectures, courses, school programs, archaeological digs and commemorations; designs exhibitions; sponsors various expeditions; and produces the "Out of the Past" radio show and cable television programs. The Society is active in furthering the arts, preserving the natural resources of The Bronx, and in creating the sense of pride in the Bronx Community.

◆

For additional information, please contact:
THE BRONX COUNTY HISTORICAL SOCIETY
3309 Bainbridge Avenue, The Bronx, New York 10467
Telephone: (212) 881-8900